Food Service Security: Internal Control

Food Service Security:
Internal Control

Bob Curtis

Chain Store Age Books
An Affiliate of Lebhar-Friedman, Inc.
New York

Food Service Security: Internal Control

Grateful acknowledgment is made to William Allen & Co., Inc., 121 W. 27 Street, New York, N. Y. 10001 for the right to reproduce the forms used in this book.

Printed in the United States of America
Library of Congress Catalog Card Number: 75-33513
International Standard Book Number: 0-912016-50-7

Contents

Acknowledgment

This book offers managers of all types of food service operations practical and proven methods for tightening their security controls against employee thefts.

The dictionary defines a *manager* as someone who has the "skill and ability to control human conduct." That is what management is all about. The problem of control is very broad and pervasive in any business. But in the food industry it is *the* major problem faced by a majority of food service operators. In fact, it is control—or the lack of it—that leads to employee thefts.

In earlier days of modern restaurant enterprise, management control presented few problems. Typically, the manager developed his own plans, directly supervised the employees who carried out those plans, and made whatever modifications were necessary. The goals of this company were identical to the goals of the proprietor. And the information needed by this top executive to run his business was minimal.

But today we are operating in a different business climate and culture. Many of these small family-type restaurants have grown into larger firms, often with separate geographical locations for their outlets. We have also seen the revolutionary birth of fast food services, with literally hundreds of outlets spread over great distances.

Now execution of the owner's and manager's plans must be performed through a hierarchy of managers, supervisors, foremen, and workers. Management needs accurate and timely information in order to determine whether controls are operating as planned. This information must come as close to a "real-time" basis as possible, so that modifications can be done at once, rather than after lengthy periods of testing and research. The longer the delay in correcting problems and deviations, the more costly the deviations become.

Over the years many improved methods have been found—usually by trial and error—for reducing the problem of internal theft. But these measures alone are still not adequate to meet the breadth and variety of larceny problems faced by food services. Today we live in a culture that has an annual increase of larceny crimes that averages 25-30 percent each year.

Many of these restaurant control methods are still incomplete or flawed. In some facilities, for example, control methods are only partial; i.e., they often concentrate on only one facet of the operation: the quality of food, cash flow, costs, or some other narrow aspect, and ignore the big picture. In others, the controls are so vast that they cannot accommodate individual needs. Managers are so busy checking on the progress of the entire operation that they can never give enough time to any one part of it that might need extra help.

A new approach to this difficult problem, however, is the measurement and control of the *employees themselves*, rather than of their output alone. The primary thrust has been to find better ways of motivating employees in order to increase the human assets of the entire company, thereby increasing its potential economic assets as well.

Only in recent years have we come to realize more and more than one of the key areas of control, both for individual segments of the restaurant and for the enterprise as a whole, is *the quality of human organization.* This area is only in its earliest stages of development. But perhaps as a result of increasing awareness and knowledge of why and how people function and work, we will be able to recognize, measure, and correct unwanted deviations in performance (such as thefts) by employees who hinder both themselves and their restaurant.

Before a manager can cope with these thefts, he must have an understanding of who steals and why. This psychological aspect of crime control has received serious attention only in most recent years. Where food service managements are aware of the security problem, planning and control are increasingly being treated as one interrelated system. Special techniques are being developed to improve the morale and performance of the enterprise as a whole, rather than dealing with individual units or divisions.

Men at the top of food service companies are now also beginning to recognize that, although vitally important to the operations, the accounting controls such as cash flow, budgets, costs, returns on investments, and so on, are "indirect" ways of controlling output. But "direct" controls—controls achieved through motivation and morale—can often pay off many times better than any external enforcement of rules. Until now, these more direct motivations have been neglected in favor of indirect controls. Today, however, while we tend to use both kinds of control, we also recognize that direct control is often a more effective way of controlling and managing a business.

This book deals with both direct and indirect controls and how you can use them to improve security. Some sections of the book are even devoted to analyzing the interpersonal situations that managers frequently have to face, and how they can act and react for maximum effectiveness: the roles they must play, the tone they should establish, the directives they must set. This brief analysis of interpersonal relationships and situations may help indicate some of the opportunities available for overcoming security problems and enhancing employee performance.

Thus the central theme of this book is the role of self-esteem in man's life. It includes the need for recognition and independence and the nature of those needs; the conditions for their fulfillment; and the consequences of frustration. Self-esteem or the lack of it has great impact on a person's values, responsibilities, goals, productivity, and honesty. Self-esteem, frustration, and employee theft are interconnecting links in the security chain.

I have written the book primarily as a conversation with an individual food service manager; with his methods, his potential, his style of management, his obligations, his values, his techniques of control, and his philosophy. The challenge to the manager is to find ways through which his subordinates can be given an opportunity for self-realization. Each person must become valued for himself, not just as another cog in a working machine. Every individual within a company must have the opportunity to grow; democracy itself rests on that growth and improvement. The purpose of management is not to threaten men into subservience; it is to free them to realize their talents as fully as possible.

If the reader is seeking a way to return to the "good old days" of the past, with the concept of controlling crime through heavy punishment of offenders, he will be disappointed. Punishment has long ago proved an untenable and ineffective approach that has only *increased* crimes and the number of criminals. Some specialists even believe that far from deterring a criminal, a prison term actually insures and may even increase the possibility of continued criminal behavior.

For over 400 years man has tried the punishment approach to solving crime. And the effect on crime rates has been the opposite of what punishment advocates have predicted. Today, we have more effective and more human ways of coping with these problems.

I cannot overstate the importance of management ideals. They mold our habits and shape our patterns of behavior. They help our managerial efforts to have significance and impact on our coworkers and on our business ability.

We learned many years ago that people cannot be held on a railroad track by standard procedures, systems memos, operating manuals. Our purposes, our practices, and our goals can only be implemented when they include the welfare of our people. Unless we as managers have concern for the people who work for us and for their needs and desires, we cannot hope to assume the responsibilities that underlie all management functions.

Like any technical book, this one has limitations. Many of the things stated in it must be accepted as a general idea or rule. To predict with complete accuracy what will be effective from a security standpoint in any one particular operation is difficult without knowing the personalities involved, the structure of the organization, operating policies and procedures, and the style of management. However, I have offered advice based on available information and on many years of experience in all facets of security and in all kinds of business operations.

Perhaps I should caution the reader that he may see himself or his company in one or more of the illustration cases throughout the text. If this does not occur, I have missed my objective, for I have tried to cover as many different kinds of situations in as many kinds of operations as possible. However, in all instances, I have disguised companies, used fictitious names, and taken precautions to preserve the confidential relationships I have with my clients. The case histories with which the reader identifies may have occurred at the opposite end of the country and in a totally different company. But the similarities and familiarities will demonstrate the universal nature of security problems in food service operations.

Naturally, this book doesn't say everything about security control. To do so would require book-length treatment of each individual subject summarized in these pages. I have tried to describe accurately and in easy-to-understand steps the methods that food service managers can apply with confidence to improve protection from internal thefts. If further information is desired, references are included in the bibliography, which I hope will help you to expand your knowledge of security control.

Perhaps most significantly, the material in this book is presented as clearly and as succinctly as possible. For this quality in the book I am deeply indebted to the creative ability of a most able writer and editor, Charles Bernstein, Executive Editor of *Nation's Restaurant News*. He undertook the formidable task of developing from a mass of raw materials I provided an easily understandable text. Not only did Charles make the material readable, but he retained my "voice"—an amazing bit of creative empathy.

I am also grateful to Julie Laitin, who did the final editing of the book. As an editor she brought logical order, clarity, and conciseness to the material. Her remarkable skill and intellectual honesty set her apart from any other editor with whom I have worked.

This book, like all of my previous books, would never have been possible without the love, patience, understanding, and creative help provided by my wife, Bette. Not only did she work hard to help me with the book, but she provided a home environment that allows for self-realization. Most of all I am grateful for her love.

No acknowledgments in anything I ever write would be complete unless I point out the contribution of Harriet Felder. Forty years ago as I sat in a high school English classroom, my teacher, Harriet Felder, lit a creative flame in my mind that she and her husband, Norman Felder, have nourished and encouraged in all the years that followed. Little that I have ever done creatively would have been possible without the training, encouragement, and inspiration of these two people.

No book such as this one represents the author's ideas and experiences alone. It is the combination of the knowledge and experience of many people. First, I am grateful to George A. Callahan, who founded the field of modern business security and who trained me in my early years of security work at Lord and Taylor's in New York City. His new concepts captured my imagination, and many of the techniques I developed over the years are based on fundamental ideas he originated. He was not only a inspiring teacher, but also a kind and patient man, always ahead of his time.

I am also deeply indebted to Dr. Fabian L. Rouke, who, until his untimely death, was considered one of the nation's leading criminal psychologists. Dr. Rouke and I worked closely together for 15 years, and he provided me the psychological training and experience on which many of my techniques have been constructed.

Also involved in early research was Dr. Ralph Benay, partner to Dr. Rouke, who served some 28 years as head psychiatrist at Sing Sing Prison, in Ossining, N.Y. Between Dr. Rouke, Dr. Benay, and me were stimulation of thought, many research studies, and experimental projects that provided fresh insights into the causes of and controls for employee thefts.

A review of the bibliography will reveal the debt I owe to many experts in a variety of related fields: such men as Dr. Carl R. Rogers, Rensis Likert, Douglas McGregor, Dr. Karl Menninger, Dr. Norman R. F. Maier, Dr. B. F. Skinner, Dr. Erik H. Erikson, Dr. Abraham H. Maslow, Dr. Hans Selye, Edward T. Hall, Dr. Donald A. Laird, Victor Lazzaro and Peter F. Drucker, among others too numerous to list.

I also want to thank Dr. Leon Weaver, head of the School of Criminal Justice, College of Social Science, Michigan State University, for his encouragement, and for the opportunities of working with him and his students as a guest lecturer in his classrooms.

At the University of Manitoba in Winnipeg, Canada, I want to thank Mr. Kenneth Galston, Assistant to the Vice President of Administration, who through our three or four counseling meetings each year over the past 10 years has proven a constant source of inspiration and help to me as a person and in my security work. I value his help and friendship, and want to note that many of the methods recommended in this volume were first tried on a field research basis under his guidance at the University of Manitoba.

No list of acknowledgments would be complete without noting the man behind this book, the man who first recognized the need for a book on this subject and then went to work to bring his mental image of such a book into reality. He is the Publishing Director of CHAIN STORE AGE BOOKS, Richard Staron.

If you have ever been told, or have ever said, "We have a security problem," or "We should do something to reduce our vulnerability to employee dishonesty," I have made every effort in this book to help you and your food service operation overcome that problem.

Bob Curtis

Foreword

The old adage "Ignorance is bliss" might be used to describe the knowledge of security which the food service industry has demonstrated in the past. Although there has been some mention of control in trade publications, security has remained a relatively unexplored area of food service management. Many food service operators, in fact, have closed their eyes to the problem entirely. However, with the changing attitudes and moral standards, particularly among younger people, it is no longer a state of bliss to remain ignorant of security problems. Managers will now find it more comfortable to develop awareness of security problems and to be confident that action is being taken to control the problems.

A few years ago, while listening to a talk on security at a restaurant convention, a speaker suggested that some restaurant employees cannot be trusted. In response, one restaurant operator got up and adamantly defended his restaurant employees. The applause which followed this defense indicated that the audience could not accept the possibility of dishonest employees in their establishments either.

One can only speculate as to why food service operators are so reluctant to face up to the realities of the problem. Obviously, it is disturbing to consider the realness and extent of dishonesty which exist in the typical restaurant. Many restaurateurs also think of themselves as artists, involved in the art of serving food, rather than as business people, involved with such matters as security control. Although all food service people have heard stories of the dishonest chef, buyer, waiter, cashier, bartender, and stock man, it is hard for them to believe that any of their loyal staff members could be guilty of such practices. Some even take it as a personal affront, rather than recognizing it as a practice of disturbed or unhappy people.

I had always believed that security was a problem for my competitors who hired "professionals," rather than for myself. I believed that my own system of hiring inexperienced people and training them in my food operation with my methods made seucrity an insignificant concern for my company. Although I would occasionally discover some incident of dishonesty, I was unaware of the importance of maintaining internal and external security controls until I read Bob Curtis' two other books, *Security Control: Internal Theft* and *Security Control: External Theft*. These books not only proved to be important influences in my business career; they actually enabled my firm to maintain a stable food cost percentage without menu price increases for almost one and one-half years, during which time the Bureau of Labor Statistics' food cost index increased more than ten percent.

In addition to discovering the extent of the losses which had been taking place, I learned about the many techniques which are available for preventing, handling, and correcting my security problems.

Mr. Curtis' previous books were aimed at the retailer. His new book, however, is designed specifically for our industry—food services. In it, he covers the problems that have plagued our particular industry for many years—including problems at the bar, commissary, and receiving rooms. Not only does he stress adequate security controls, but he also makes us aware of how important employee training, counseling, and morale building are in diminishing employee dishonesty.

As we begin to adopt new techniques for security control, we will experience dramatic improvements in our operations. We will not only reduce the shortages which we may be taking for granted, but we can also discover pitfalls we had not known about before. We will develop a new awareness of potential leaks in receiving, storage, issuing of merchandise, checking sales, collecting cash, and balancing registers.

Moreover, this book will help uncover incidents of dishonesty, explain how to establish guilt, and tell you how to conduct an interrogation interview that makes it possible to determine the extent of security problems while protecting your restaurant from liability.

Bob Curtis' books have become required reading for my own managers. Since I have established this requirement, they have a new sense of awareness. Our monthly meetings now include a discussion on the subject of security, and from these discussions have come many improvements in our training and controls. The new emphasis on security has brought a spirit of mutual respect, trust, and security, which in turn has improved employee morale. The savings I have realized through improved security has enabled me to be more competitive in my menu prices and in compensating my employees.

This book can be a training aid for management staff to guide and improve security controls. It is encouraging to know that we will have this new aid in exploring a relatively new area of food service business management. I am confident that we as an industry will be making even greater progress in the direction of reducing our losses due to dishonesty. Savings gained through improved security will improve our competitive positions and our employee relations.

I look upon the publication of *Food Service Security: Internal Control* as the beginning of a new era for the food service industry; an era in which the industry will grow in strength, understanding, and ability; an era in which it will adopt more modern and effective business techniques, while insuring that the preparation and service of food remain an art.

Harry H. Pope
President
H. A. Pope & Sons, Inc.
Pope's Cafeterias
St. Louis, Missouri

PART 1

Introduction

1

Dimensions of the Problem

The blonde, blue-eyed waitress was one of the most trusted employees in a small Portland, Oregon restaurant. She had worked there for five years and was known for her courtesy, friendliness, and excellent performance. She was the ideal employee.

Or so it seemed . . . until one day the owner became suspicious when he noticed that he always seemed to have fewer soup spoons on hand than he thought he had. So he decided to question his employees about the mysterious disappearances. This is when he discovered that the innocent-looking waitress whom he trusted so much had been tossing spoons out the back door of the restaurant for quite a while. And she wasn't doing it as a favor to get rid of any bad silverware.

Instead, at 7 o'clock each evening her boyfriend appeared in the alley behind the restaurant's rear window. The waitress would slip the spoons out to him in between her trips to and from her customers. After making sure that nobody was watching, her boyfriend slid the items under his jacket and sauntered casually out into sidewalk traffic. Neither the manager nor the customers suspected that the waitress with the winning smile was dishonest.

Sadly enough, this scene is repeated daily with a different cast and slightly altered actions. Some employees drop meats and canned goods out of windows for friends to retrieve. Others wrap food in aluminum, drop it in the garbage can, and pick it up on the way home. Still others conceal candy, china, liquor, food, and cigarettes in their pockets, in large handbags, in or under coats. Some give away free meals; others undercharge their friends. These are all forms of theft found in restaurants from coast to coast.

In the case of the blonde, blue-eyed waitress, as in so many cases, the owner had closed his eyes to the situation for too long. Why? Probably because he suspected that someone was stealing, and if his suspicions were confirmed, he would have to fire that person. The idea of firing a trusted employee, especially one like the waitress, was a nightmare to him. He had come to look upon her as more than just another worker. He felt that she kept things running efficiently and was someone he could trust. But finally he had to face facts. The figures in his ledgers didn't jibe. And he couldn't continue to absorb the mounting shortages reflected in his accounts.

Like this man, many food service owners are undermining everything they've worked so hard to achieve because they fail to act on problems as soon as they are alerted to them. Robberies and burglaries of restaurants and other businesses have soared to record proportions. But internal theft—aided by restaurant owners' own acts of omission—is the number one problem for restaurant owners and operators.

Profits Siphoned Off

In a single recent year the U.S. Department of Commerce estimated a total of $16 billion in business losses from reported employee thefts. And this estimate did not even include the losses from unreported thefts. Even more alarming, of businesses that failed that year, employee theft was listed as the major cause in 34% of the cases.

Restaurants have one of the highest failure rates of any industry, and one of the chief reasons is employee theft. Often this is because of careless management, although in difficult economic times, dips in the number of customers cause some closings. In depressed times, however, extra care and watchfulness are particularly important.

How serious can the results be of carelessness in watching for theft? One Indiana seafood restaurant lost $80,000 (over 10% of sales) during a 10-month period from a combination of employee thefts and embezzlement at top levels. It's no coincidence that a management which initiates such activities in its own ranks finds its employees acting dishonestly also. This pervasive laxity and immorality led directly to the restaurant's closing. And the same story is repeated all too often in restaurants throughout the U.S.

Although the food service industry has recently grown in professionalism and size, many restaurant operators still haven't learned enough about managing their own businesses. This is confirmed by the fact that over 50% of industry profits are being lost through errors, carelessness, and thefts. Paradoxically, restaurateurs who show great enterprise in building up their businesses have been unable to control a problem as basic as employee theft. Perhaps this is because they have not wanted to acknowledge that the problem is as serious and as widespread as it is. However, those who have recognized the problem and tackled it early have been rewarded with better employee morale and higher profits.

The prevalence of theft by employees is a fact of life that many businessmen find difficult to accept. Employee theft accounts for about 75% of a restaurant's inventory shortages. Paperwork mistakes and external losses account for the remainder of shortages. One study showed that three of every four employees in a particular group had stolen more than $100 in merchandise or cash. And each of these thefts had occurred in the six months prior to the study.

Collusion among employees is also becoming a common practice. In one restaurant chain's warehouse, six receiving managers, in collusion with 12 truck drivers, looted a warehouse of about $2 million in food items before being discovered.

Damage to Profits

Employee thefts magnify losses well beyond the specific amounts stolen. All theft losses come out of *net profits*. This means that a resturant that makes a 3% net profit but suffers a 1% shortage has in fact lost a full one-third, or 33%, of its hard-earned profits. We tend to think of losses in terms of percentages of *sales*. Actually, rather than sales, they are directly related to profits.

A restaurant with $500,000 in annual sales that finds a 1% shortage has not merely lost the $5,000 that a 1% shortage suggests. It has also lost all the profits on all the food that must be sold to pay for this shortage. In this case it would mean selling $170,000 worth of food without any profit at all in order to pay for the $5,000 shortage. Many restaurants are forced to operate without profit from two to four months each year to pay for their losses.

It's gotten to the point where many restaurants lose more money and food items from internal theft than they can make in net profits. Often they have to set aside as much as 1%-2% of sales as a reserve to cover theft losses.

When a sagging economy and inflation bite into profits, many restaurants have to struggle under the twin burdens of higher food costs and lower customer counts. With the pressure on bottom line profits growing increasingly intense, it's more important than ever to maintain a careful security watch.

Serious Consequences

Besides the damage to profits, internal theft results in other costly consequences. Among the most serious:

• The loss of valued employees whom you have spent a great deal of time to train.

• Heavy costs needed to train new employees to replace the ones who are gone.

• A lowering of morale all over the restaurant when suspicion is focused on an employee who had been considered honest and valuable.

• The contamination of other employees who may justify their own thefts by pointing out peers who are doing the same thing.
• Possible loss of important and irreplaceable records through theft.
• Bad publicity which can damage a restaurant's image.

In both emotional and financial terms, thefts cause loss and harm to individuals and to businesses.

Society As Instigator

The problem of security appears to be becoming more serious. Part of the reason for this is the rapid acceleration of change in our society. Economic and psychological changes occur at rates that some people cannot cope with or understand.

President Johnson's Crime Commission in the mid-1960's, of which I was a part, conducted studies that traced some of these changes back to the early 1950's. At that time, many people began to change their outlooks. Rather than relying on their own inner strengths and moral beliefs, many people began relying on others as indicators of right and wrong. This meant that they could justify their behavior on the basis of other people's behaving in similar fashion.

Thus, if a cashier discovered her boss stealing, it is possible that he or she would feel justified in doing the same thing. This is one of the reasons that stealing is so dangerous. Often it becomes contagious.

Your Responsibilities As a Restaurant Operator

Almost everyone is tempted to steal at one time or another. If these temptations are realized, the consequences are painful for both the restaurant management and the employee. Accusations can and usually do harm an individual and his family. Even questioning an individual may connote guilt. Confronting a trusted employee with a charge of dishonesty and theft is not a pleasant task; it is one that can be avoided with the proper preventive measures.

It is your responsibility as a restaurant operator to make sure that such temptations are not realized. This can be done by setting up systems to combat internal theft and implement methods of keeping employees honest. Good management skills, careful personnel screening, maintaining high employee morale and avoiding potential problems before they start all contribute to success in this area.

PART 2
Basic Safeguards

PART 2

Basic Safeguards

2

Screening Prospective Employees

Suave, 34-year-old Bill Smith sat down in a restaurant owner's office one day and explained the kind of job he would like to do as an assistant manager. The more Smith talked, the more confident the restaurateur became that this indeed was just the man for the job. Smith seemed bright, clean-cut, and aggressive. And he appeared to be telling the truth about his successes and achievements at his other jobs. There seemed to be no reason to waste time checking Smith's background.

Just to make sure, however, the restaurateur decided to give the well-polished applicant a pro forma polygraph lie detector test. Smith passed it and was immediately hired. Unfortunately, food items started disappearing shortly after Smith began working, and three weeks later the owner checked with Smith's previous employers. He discovered that Smith was a compulsive thief. Even worse, he had infected some of the other employees at his latest restaurant with the same tendency during his short stay.

How could this have happened? Actually the restaurant owner had not emphasized the proper precautions. The only care he had taken in screening this applicant was to administer a polygraph test. These tests are far from foolproof, and the result caused harm to both the restaurant owner and his employees.

You may someday have to face—and perhaps you already have—a situation like this in your own restaurant operation. The easiest way to avoid such a problem is to be particularly careful in your prehiring stages. This can save you untold trouble, loss, and heartache.

Personnel Screening

What is personnel screening? It is checking every angle about the person so carefully that when you hire him, you are reasonably sure he is honest and the right person for the job. Once you have hired enough honest and capable people, you can turn your attention to direct methods of increasing your company's profits rather than to ways of combating internal theft on the premises. Yet many food service companies are too casual about screening applicants and watching for warning signals. Oddly enough, the same person who would never think of placing a bet on a horse without carefully checking its past performance record, thinks nothing of hiring a person without doing any investigation whatever of his background or character.

Far too many people rely on externals alone to evaluate the honesty of a person. No matter how unscientific or biased their judgment may be, they believe that if a person looks presentable and speaks well, he is undoubtedly honest. But we must keep in mind that every dishonest person who is discovered on our staff was selected and hired by our company. In too many cases, we should have known better.

Few people become dishonest all of a sudden. Usually they have left clues around for months or even for years which, if recognized, would have tipped us off that something was wrong. How often is a dishonest employee interrogated, only to discover that facts were revealed in his employment interview or on his employment card that should have indicated that he was a poor risk in the first place? His character is as apparent as if he had written "I AM A THIEF" in large letters across the face of the application. Many times, we also notice warning signs during the employment interview, but we may ignore them or rationalize them by saying to ourselves: "He did that a long time ago. It is none of our business. I am only concerned about the type of person he is today and tomorrow; I am not really interested in his past."

Another problem is that we don't know what to look for. We may overlook valuable clues because of weaknesses in our selection process, carelessness, or lack of knowledge. We simply don't check out certain provable statements or claims made by the person seeking employment.

Naturally, everyone who screens personnel wants to do a good job, but occasionally time limitations or the demands of people who need extra help force us to put the applicant's integrity and honesty at the bottom of our list of priorities. Yet, the backbone of every business is its people. If we fail to put character and integrity among the first requirements for any position in the company, we are making a basic mistake in concept which can be costly to the store and to every person who works there.

Upgrading the screening of new employees is probably the single most important safeguard for preventing internal theft. It is understandable, of course, that the person doing the screening is often primarily concerned with finding an individual capable of doing the job. What is difficult to comprehend is that so many restaurants and food service operations appear to be completely *unaware* that honesty is even a factor for consideration at the point of employment. This is an attitude that does considerable disservice to the restaurant. Such negligence of a fundamental security control can be extremely costly.

But how do you screen a person applying for a job? What factors do you look for? What are the sources of your information? How should you go about doing it? Over the years, professional security men have developed several methods that have proven successful in screening out high-risk candidates at the point of employment. Hundreds of food service operations across the country have upgraded their personnel and have substantially reduced internal theft by using these simple screening measures. Your restaurant can do the same. The techniques require a bit of knowledge and effort; but taken one step at a time, none of them is arduous or difficult to master. Further, they pay off handsomely in providing your restaurant with a mature and capable staff.

Seven Important Character Traits

Not everyone you hire must be dynamic and aggressive. In fact, it's quite important that most of your staff have particular inner qualities that may not be immediately perceived by the casual onlooker. But in the long run, an employee with seven basic character traits should prove honest and reliable. The seven characteristics you should be looking for are:

1. *A positive attitude.* This means that when you assign an employee a task, he or she does it willingly and enthusiastically.
2. *Enthusiasm and drive.* This will give an employee the energy and outlook needed to do the job well.
3. *Persistence.* An individual with persistence will stick to a task until it is done, will be able to cope with some of the frustration that comes up in any job, and will complete whatever job he or she sets out to do.
4. *Maturity.* A person with maturity will probably also have a sense of responsibility and integrity. This means handling the pressures, disappointments, and satisfactions of the job with presence and equanimity.
5. *Skill.* You will also want an employee who has a developed skill or native ability for a particular kind of work for which he or she is interviewing.
6. *Tact.* In most cases it is quite important that an employee have the ability to work and get along with others. This is particularly true in the restaurant field, where employees are constantly dealing with other people.
7. *Integrity.* The employee with integrity will have a sense of moral and personal pride in himself and in his work that will make him or her a trusted and respected member of the staff.

These traits—especially the last—are the important qualities to look for in potential employees. A person with these traits is likely to be a successful employee; one who will be a major asset to you and to your restaurant; one who is likely to give you help and satisfaction. However, these are qualities that are difficult to determine from a casual screening or from an initial impression. Therefore, a careful and complete screening is necessary to make sure that a person meets most of the criteria.

Look for Evidence of Past Dishonestry

Recent Supreme Court rulings having suggested that we can no longer ask "Have you ever been arrested?" on the employment application form. This question was first challenged when one large industrial organization turned down a black job applicant who had recently graduated from college. On the employment application the question was asked, "Have you ever been arrested?" The applicant told the interviewer that the form didn't have enough space to list all his arrests. He went on to explain that white people don't understand ghetto life; whenever there's trouble, the police arrest everyone in sight. He stated that he was never even tried, just detained a few hours or a day and then released. He admitted he had been arrested 13 or 14 times for "suspicion of theft," "suspicion of housebreaking," and so on.

The interviewer rejected the applicant. As a result, the man appealed to a civil rights group, charging the company with racial discrimination. The argument presented was that it is common knowledge that blacks are arrested without justification more frequently than whites. He claimed that the question about arrests is designed to screen out minority-group applicants. The company replied that it felt it had the right not to hire anyone with an arrest record, whether he was black or white.

The case went to the U.S. District Court, and the court held that the question concerning arrest is unfair and must be dropped from employment applications. "Excluding from jobs persons who have suffered a number of arrests without any conviction is unlawful. It has the effect of denying black applicants equal opportunity for employment." The point to keep in mind here is that an arrest is not proof of guilt. The interviewer should concern himself only with convictions.

But even rejection on the basis of criminal conviction may soon be made unlawful. Courts and agencies appear to be heading toward a ruling that minority-group members cannot be denied jobs even if convicted, assuming the convictions are merely for youthful offenses or other "minor" crimes. What they will define as "minor" crimes will be an important guide in the screening process of job applicants. Thus, the present situation allows you to reject an applicant on the basis of a conviction for a crime against property, but not for an arrest on a "suspicion" of larceny.

Although this arrest question appears to be illegal at present, there is still no reason why the person in charge of employment should not make a reasonable effort to check out a candidate's past record of behavior. This is probably one of the most important screening controls we have. A person who has been involved in larceny is a poor risk in a restaurant where food items and money are easy to take. Larcenists will generally repeat their theft patterns on and off for the rest of their lives unless they receive some type of psychological help or are placed in a working environment where there is little opportunity for theft.

No one should be hired unless you have checked to see if he has a previous criminal conviction for larceny. Look particularly for any convictions for crimes against property, such as shoplifting, automobile theft, burglary, and robbery. Employing a person with this type of background must be weighed carefully, because it is often unfair to the company and unfair to the applicant to place him in a position of temptation.

Is it possible for a person with a police record to be a good risk? Couldn't he have learned his lesson and gone straight? Unfortunately the evidence in support of this view is not encouraging. Studies by criminal psychologists, security specialists, and the federal government have shown that people who are arrested for various larceny offenses often repeat their crimes. The Federal Bureau of Investigation, for example, began studying the problem of repeating offenders back in 1963. In one of its first studies, it followed the careers of 17,837 individuals who were released by the court and penal institutions in 1963. The record of rearrest for these offenders in the 30 months from the date of their release was as follows:

—Of those released after serving a prison term, 67 percent had been rearrested.

—Of those released on parole, 75 percent had been rearrested.

—Of those acquitted or dismissed by the courts, 83 percent had been rearrested.

These figures are startling. The evidence is clear that most applicants with a police conviction for theft are a poor employment risk in a restaurant.

What if the man or woman got in trouble several years ago and hasn't been in trouble since? If the person was very young at the time of the theft incident, this should be considered. Many teenagers go through a stage in which they steal; but since no criminal pathology is involved, they don't become adult criminals. But do not be misled by the fact that a person of 39, arrested at the age of 24 and not again, is necessarily a good risk. The chances of apprehending a thief a second time are extremely low. Police, at the present time, are apprehending only 18 percent of the individuals involved in reported larcenies. This means that the chances of a reported larcenist escaping arrest favor the criminal by 82 percent.

If an applicant admits that he has stolen previously and even admits he has served time in prison, isn't that a good sign? Do not assume that such a person automatically becomes a good risk because he seems to be truthful about his police record. He may have confessed his past thefts because he feels you already know about them or that your investigation before hiring him will uncover the truth anyway. He is therefore putting his best foot for forward by appearing to admit his past "mistakes." Surprisingly enough, many people who hire personnel are misled into believing that frankness about a previous criminal record is proof positive that the person is basically an "honest" person.

Rehabilitation Is Not a Wise Gamble

There's a well-known large restaurant in New York City that insists on interviewing only men who have worked in the coal mines of Pennsylvania when it hires busboys or counter-men. The thinking is that men who have been conditioned to the most strenuous type work will take naturally and without complaint to the hard work necessary in a restaurant.

This very point is why it is so crucial to check so carefully on an applicant's entire past record. I'm convinced that people basically don't change much. By the time a person is 12 years old, almost all his behavior patterns have been formed, and these same patterns will continue through adulthood.

You yourself may be able to think of some people you have known for some time. There's a good likelihood that if you have known these people over a long period of time, they are today much as they were many years ago, just as they will probably be similar in their drives and temperaments many years from now.

Behavior patterns are so deeply rooted that it is unlikely they will change except under extreme adversity or through intensive counseling. To expect any significant changes in a person you're hiring is unrealistic. If you want a strong leader, choose a man who is already a strong leader. It is generally unwise to hire a more passive individual who claims he will develop into a more assertive person. Similarly, if you want someone who prefers to leave the decision-making process to others, then hire a less aggressive person. Just be sure that the character and qualities of the person you hire fit the needs of the particular job from the moment he starts. Any efforts to change his character require so much time that they're generally not worth it.

Check with the Local Police Department

In some cities, restaurateurs check job applicants for a previous criminal record through the local police department. To do this, they provide the police with the full name of the person, his address, and his date of birth. If the applicant is female, then both her maiden name and married name should also be included. In other cities, local legal ordinances forbid the police to check out applicants. As a way around this situation, some stores provide the applicant with an "inquiry form" to take to the police station. After the police sign the form, stating that the individual does not have a record of criminal conviction, he returns it to the employment office. Although local law may forbid the restaurant to check on a person's criminal record, it usually allows the person to do so himself.

It is also wise to check with the police in those cities in which the applicant lived during the past 10 years. There are three ways in which you can do this: 1) Ask a member of your police department to check out this information through his police contacts in the other cities. 2) Hire a local detective agency to make this check. Select one that belongs to a national association to insure that it has contacts in those cities from which the information must be obtained. The fee is nominal. 3) Use a letter of inquiry to out-of-town police departments giving the subject's name, address, the dates when he lived in the city, and his date of birth. Be sure to include a self-addressed, stamped envelope for the reply. While police in some areas will not be cooperative, this is not universally true, and every attempt should be made to obtain such information on criminal convictions.

Speak with Past Employers

Most employment specialists raise considerable question as to the value of personal references listed on an employment application. "What purpose do they serve?" they ask. "The reply will be watered down by kindness, forgetfulness, negligence, or a fear of committing oneself to some type of situation which may later prove embarrassing."

As real as these problems are, the case for checking references remains impressive. A systematic reference check and a skillful analysis of the information returned are good sources for evaluating the applicant's character, dependability, cooperativeness, level of production, and particularly his integrity and honesty. Further, the word gets around that your restaurant checks references, and job applicants will be less inclined to give you false information.

To help you avoid the pitfalls of doing a personal reference check with the applicant's previous employers, conduct the check by telephone or in person, rather than by mail. Conversation allows you to ask additional questions, and it yields more specific details than does a written reply. People are reluctant to put certain information into writing, particularly anything that is derogatory. If the former employer feels that the applicant is an honesty risk, he is more likely to say so or to hint at his suspicions on the phone. If he turns out to be reasonably frank, however, and states quite directly that he believes the employee is dishonest, then you can try to pin him down to specifics. What particular evidence does he have that led to his conclusion? Obviously, the most useful information will be obtained when you are personally known to the individual you are calling.

Sometimes when you do a reference check of previous employers, you find that the applicant has lied about his past job experience. He may never have worked for the firm, or you may find that the company he listed doesn't even exist. Uncovering these facts is important. Such lies are of sufficient magnitude to indicate that the applicant should be rejected.

Whether you check a person by telephone, by mail, or by talking to his former employer in person, try to contact all the companies the applicant has worked for during the past ten years. Keep in mind that a sufficient length of time must be covered to make certain that the many facets of his personality have been properly considered. Clinical psychologists have observed that flaws in personality structure may appear infrequently, and by limiting the reference check to a brief period of time, say the last few months, you may fail to disclose important information that occurred periodically in past years.

It is also important to keep your investigation broad in scope. Obtain information from people who have seen the candidate in a variety of situations. It's a good idea, for example, to seek information not only from the owner or manager of another restaurant in which an individual worked, but from someone he worked with, such as a colleague or a subordinate.

Evaluate Your Reference Sources

Because the sources you contact will evaluate the candidate in general or subjective terms, such references have limited value. They do, of course, give you some insight into how the person sees the applicant, but it's more productive if you can pin down these evaluations by asking for specifics. In other words, ask the reference how he arrived at his evaluation. If he gives you a negative report, you must determine if his attitude is biased. Perhaps there had been a personality clash or some other incident which resulted in his negative conclusions. His views may not be proven valid by the evidence at hand.

Don't forget you are not only rating the man applying for the job, but you are evaluating the person supplying the reference. As you talk with him, determine how objective he is. Does he seem to be biased in his viewpoint about this person? What standards does he use for making this type of evaluation? Does he seem to know his family or his hobbies, for example? Did the applicant work directly under the man with whom you are talking, or does he know him only through hearsay?

It sometimes helps if you prepare a list of questions in advance. In that way, you can get the information you want without later finding out that you have omitted something important from your telephone or in-person inquiry. Naturally, you should feel free to depart from your checklist whenever answers open up new leads. The checklist is only to give you some guidelines to follow so that you are certain to touch upon all of the important questions. Here are a few points to be considered:

1. What were the dates of his employment?
2. What was his salary?
3. What were his duties on the previous job?
4. Was he a person of integrity and honesty?

5. What sort of record did he have for illness? Tardiness? Did he have any compensation claims against the company?
6. How cooperative and dependable was he?
7. Did he show initiative and ambition on the job? Was he hard working? Productive? A self-starter?
8. What were his relations with his associates? With his boss? How did they feel about him? Was he a loner? Did he drink a lot alone or with the gang after work? What sort of person was he exactly?
9. Would you rehire him? If not, why not?

If you are the manager or owner of a food service operation, don't hesitate to delegate this reference-checking job to the man in charge of the area in which this particular worker will be assigned. After all, the department head should have a strong personal interest in hiring the right person for the job, so place some responsibility on him for selecting the employee. He is going to be careful in screening the applicant and in making his evaluation.

Wherever possible, try to check references *before* you put a person on the job. In order to speed up the hiring process, some companies postpone such screenings until after a person is employed. This is a risky procedure. In many cases, major thefts and the corruption of other honest employees have occurred in the two or three weeks between the time the person is assigned to work and the time the employment person discovers his criminal record. So try to screen the applicant *before* you put him to work.

Determine the Person's Financial Situation

Is the applicant under any unusual financial pressure? Does he owe payment on a lot of bills? Has he ever been brought into court for nonpayment of debts? Has his salary ever been garnisheed? Make it a routine practice to get a credit bureau report on each person before hiring him. Credit bureaus today have considerable information. The Associated Credit

Bureaus of America, for example, has records on 120 million people.

Today's credit bureau files contain a lot more than a list of the cars and cameras purchased on credit. They tell you if a person owns his own home, what kind of furniture he has, whether he has passed bad checks, and so on. They also include newspaper clippings, records of lawsuits, data on police actions against him, and items of this nature. These reports, therefore, can often provide valuable background material to help you evaluate the applicant's past performance in terms of his record of personal integrity and honesty.

Conduct a Neighborhood Investigation

When the person being hired is going to be put into a critical job, such as head of the cash flow, some restaurants make it a point to have a trained investigator talk to some of the people in the applicant's neighborhood. If such an investigation seems warranted, the investigator should talk to the neighbors either in person or by telephone to find out if there is any indication that the applicant is a poor risk. For example, is he known to be living beyond his means? Does he have undesirable associates? Does he have a reputation as a "heavy drinker?" Is he known to be a chronic gambler? Does he have a reputation for immoral conduct? Is he heavily in debt? An unfavorable report on any of these six factors should cause the person doing the screening to think twice before hiring this person for a job in a place where the supervision is minimal and the opportunity to steal is maximum.

Use a Bonding Company Application Form

Many restaurants have the job applicant make out a bonding company form as well as an employment application blank. The person with a previous criminal record is frequently more concerned about the bonding application than he is about the employment card. He is aware that bonding companies usually make an investigation into the background of individuals before approving them. If the applicant has a previous criminal record, he may feel that the bonding company will surely uncover it and report it to the restaurant. As a result, when the bonding company form is used, the dishonest applicant frequently does not return for his second interview. He thus screens himself out of the job.

For the same reason, a few firms today also fingerprint and photograph applicants. This is largely used as a psychological device to scare off the person who has a criminal record. Of course, this tactic may provoke an undesirable reaction on the part of an honest applicant. Such procedures have too many overtones of a "police state." Therefore, you have to judge the advisability of this approach on the basis of the location of the restaurant, the type of image it projects to the community, and the quality or type of individual it seeks to employ.

Most people, however, even those who are sensitive to any action that reflects on their integrity, do not resent a bonding company form; and for the most part the bonding company form is just as effective a psychological device as are the techniques of fingerprinting and photographing the applicant. It is certainly less traumatic for the honest person.

Review the Employment Application

Frequently the man doing the hiring looks over the application form without really knowing exactly what he is looking for. Most employment applications provide for a listing of previous jobs in order of dates of employment. This listing is extremely important to the interviewer. He should look carefully down the dates of employment to see if there are any gaps in the person's employment record. When he discovers such a gap, he should ask for an explanation. The answer given by the applicant may sound extremely logical. He may say: "I was in business for myself for a year selling storm windows. But I found that I couldn't make a go of it and had to go back to my former line of work." Or he may say he visited relatives in Europe that year, and so on. But no matter what the story is or how logical it sounds, it is extremely important for the interviewer to postpone any decision on hiring this person until he can do a factual check on the applicant's story.

More often than not, he will find that he has discovered a clue to trouble in the person's employment background. It may be that he worked for another company and was discharged for dishonesty, so he has omitted that period on his employment listing, hoping the interviewer won't notice it. In some cases, it has been found that the applicant was actually serving time in jail during the period when his application shows a gap in employment. So check out his story and get the facts.

It is also common sense to check out any claims that can be investigated. If a story contains specific details, then these can be verified by talking to the people involved. Particularly important are the simple factual checks that can be made during the interview itself. For instance if the applicant says he was recently discharged from the army, ask him to show you his discharge papers; ask him also for a copy of his school graduation records, and so on. It is a good habit not to accept the applicant's word alone when the factual material can be easily requested and examined during the interview.

Watch for the Psychotic Person

The most dangerous type of thief is the "psychotic" or the "criminally minded" person. He is the most dangerous because once he becomes a member of the staff, little can be done to prevent him from stealing. His thefts are invariably large, but, what is worse, he often coerces normally honest employees to steal in order to protect himself. It also does little good to try to screen out this type of individual by using a lie detector test. A psychopath's personality is characterized by an abnormal lack of fear, so he can often pass a polygraph screening test with a clean record. Because the lie detector works on fear reactions, the test indicates he is a good employee risk, as it did for Bill Smith. Only later does management realize the extent of its error, and usually it is too late to undo the damage.

Fortunately, however, researchers have developed tests to screen out such abnormally delinquent applicants. One which has proven effective is called a "Personnel Reaction" test. It was developed by Dr. Harrison Gough, Jr., Head of the Psychology Department at the University of California, Berkeley Division. The test consists of 64 questions which sound harmless to the applicant and give no indication that they are meant to reveal delinquency. Some of the typical questions on this test are:

"Have you ever wanted to run away and join a circus?"
"Are you afraid of deep water?"
"Does a rainstorm frighten you?"
"Have you ever been afraid of being in a car wreck?"
"Does the thought of certain animals make you nervous?"
"Do you frequently have bad dreams or nightmares?"

In a field study of this test, a few years ago, 830 part-time Christmas employees hired in November by a store in New York City were given Dr. Gough's "Personnel Reaction" test. The unrated tests were placed in a locked desk until February when all the temporary employees had left the company. At that time the tests were rated, and the results showed that 72 of the employees in that group were "delinquent." Although the store had a small security staff of only nine detectives who devoted the major part of their work to apprehending shoplifters, they had, nevertheless, apprehended 36 of the 72 employees rated delinquent by Dr. Gough's test. Through the use of such tests, this insidious criminal type can be identified before he unleashes his aggression on your store.

Whether or not you use formal tests of this kind, by including questions in the interview that relate to the applicant's fears, you can often learn whether the person exhibits a normal range of fear reactions, or whether he appears to have psychotic tendencies. If there is any indication that the latter may be the case, and you are interested in hiring the person, then it would be wise to have him tested by a competent psychologist.

Be Alert to Giveaway Gestures

There is considerable interest today in how people reveal themselves through gestures. Although we may say one thing verbally, sometimes we are saying something quite different with our gestures. Interviewers should be sensitive to giveaway gestures during the job interview, and should try to uncover with further questions why a particular topic elicited such a reaction. The matter may not be significant, but it should be looked into. Here are a few gestures the skilled interviewer should watch for:

1. When a man passes his hand over his face while talking, usually when answering a question, this may mean that he wants to evade the issue under discussion. If you ask him, for example, "How did you get along with your previous boss?" and he rubs his face or passes his hands over his eyes before he says "Just great!" you can suspect that he would rather not tell you the real truth about the relationship.

2. If he crushes his cigarette violently or draws a doodle with unusual force, perhaps breaking the point of his pencil, this may mean that underneath an apparently calm exterior lies a very hostile and angry person.

3. During the discussion, if the subject becomes excited and bangs on the desk or shouts for emphasis, this often reveals an inward awareness that he is not telling the truth or that he believes his pretenses are being found out by the interviewer. The loudness of the argument and the violence of the pounding indicate a defensive attitude which has serious implications in the interview situation.

4. If he rubs his nose while answering a question or during the discussion, this may reflect a personal dissatisfaction with what is being said in the conversation. Watch for this sign particularly when salary is being discussed.

5. Itching and scratching may mean embarrassment or excitement and can indicate a person with an extremely low threshold of nervous control.

6. A sudden loss of color from the face is frequently a sign that the person has been asked something that frightens him. Usually signs of fear will appear in clusters. The

applicant's mouth will suddenly go dry, and you will notice that his tongue touches his lips to moisten them before he speaks. In fact, the corners of his mouth may even firm up as though he were eating a lemon, a reflex reaction caused by fear.

7. Excessive sweating by the applicant may indicate extreme anxiety.

Ask Probing Questions

To be effective, the interview with the applicant should range across several areas of his life. Questions should cover such topics as his education, his previous type of work, and his financial situation. Does he own his own home? What part of the city does he live in? What sort of hobbies does he have? How is his general health? You will also want to discuss his military service, what he did in the armed forces, and so on. Dig into any other matters that are directly related to the points you are concerned about. Why did he leave his last job? What is his family background? What are his hobbies and personal interests, his marital status, his personal aspirations and ambitions, and his previous income? Has he ever received workmen's compensation for an injury?

Ask other questions which will determine how stable his employment pattern has been in the past. Does he appear to be a man who hops from job to job or does he stay in one job for a considerable length of time? What has motivated him in the past to move from one position to another? Is he an overly dependent person? Is he a person with strong ambitions and drive? What sort of home life did he have as a child? What is his home life like today? Is he a stable person? Does he seem to be a drifter? Is he a man who agrees with watever you say or is he a person with individual opinions? Are his opinions logical or emotional?

One characteristic that you must probe for, in particular, is the maturity of the person. Can he stand up under frustration?

How does he handle his problems? Does he find that small incidents upset him? Is he mature enough to have developed techniques for avoiding frustrations, going around them, or working his way through them?

Because his ability to handle frustration is directly related to his risk level in the retail store, be sure to learn what his earning aspirations are. If they are too high in terms of the job for which you are considering him, then watch out! Chances are that he will soon become extremely frustrated in this job, and these feelings may lead to theft.

Another very important aspect of the interview is to find out what he thinks about the relative honesty of people in general. Most of us tend to believe that other people are like ourselves. For example, if we take a group of executives at random and say to them, "What percentage of the employees in the store do you think steal?" one executive will say 1 percent, another will say 10 percent, and another will say 20 percent. These estimates usually indicate that the person is himself relatively honest and therefore finds it difficult to believe that many people steal. On the other hand, if the executive says 75 percent or 85 percent steal, or if he says that 98 percent steal, then the interviewer should be careful. Chances are that this person is dishonest—we usually see ourselves in others.

The interviewer should also be alert to any indication of cheating or dishonesty on the part of the person being questioned, particularly any contradictions or discrepancies in the applicant's answers. He must take nothing for granted and must closely question those people who show any subtle indication of deceit. For example, these would be people who:

1. cough, stammer, or hesitate before answering a question
2. have ready-made alibis for rationalizing unfavorable reports, have glib explanations for gaps in their employment records, or who talk too easily, too rapidly, and too smoothly
3. go into long and detailed descriptions about previous work experience and earnings
4. give evidence of living or dressing beyond their income.

Here is a list of ten questions that can help you cover a person's interests and abilities effectively:

1. If you could create the perfect job for yourself, what would it be?
2. In what jobs or capacities do you feel you have been most effective?
3. What untapped resources do you feel you have that you could use in this job?
4. What do you consider to be your best qualities on the job?
5. What do you consider to be your main weaknesses?
6. How do you react to criticism?
7. Have you ever supervised the work of others? If so, how did you find the experience?
8. How would you say you get along with others?
9. How would you say you work with others?
10. How is your health?

Evaluate the Applicant's Intelligence

Studies over the years have proven repeatedly that there is a relationship between intelligence and honesty. These studies show that a person with better-than-average intelligence is generally more likely to be honest than a person of lower intelligence.

There is usually an optimum intelligence level for most jobs. The restaurateur embarking on the use of intelligence tests is wise to test people who have worked for him successfully for several years in order to determine what the optimum level is for their particular jobs. By identifying the intelligence levels of present employees, you will establish useful guidelines for selecting individuals to fill the same or similar positions. Applicants scoring in the quarter of ratings below that level are probably going to be slow to learn the work, and they are going to be inaccurate. On the other hand, those who are in the top quarter may become restless, bored, and frustrated.

From the point of view of honesty, it is sound business to try to hire only those applicants who achieve at least the average level in the optimum intelligence standard set for each particular type of job. Those with lower-than-average scores are greater security risks, depending, of course, on how far down the intelligence scale they are and on the temptations to steal offered by the position.

Although the use of an intelligence test is highly recommended, it is not always convenient to use this approach. However, the interviewer can soon determine the relative range of an applicant's intelligence by such means as listening to how well the person speaks, reviewing his schooling, or finding out what he reads.

For example, if the applicant expresses himself clearly and is able to use words with abstract meanings, this is a sign of intelligence. The applicant who has finished high school should possess at least a low-average intelligence level. If he graduated high in his class, he will be either at the high-average or superior intelligence level. The person who graduated from college is probably at the superior level, depending upon the standards of the college.

By discussing the candidate's preferences in reading matter, you can also sometimes judge his intelligence level. Ascertain what newspapers or books the employee reads. Is he a comic book fan? Does he read sophisticated literary journals? His reading tastes can reveal much about his intellectual capacity.

When forming your personal estimate of an applicant's intelligence, be careful to avoid the pitfalls that can mislead you in making an accurate assessment. We are constantly taking the measure of people around us by their appearance. The intelligence of a good-looking and well-dressed person is usually overrated, while that of a less attractive person is generally underrated. These outward qualities tell us nothing aout their brain power.

Also, be careful of misjudging people who have a singular talent or one major accomplishment. Outstanding athletes, musicians, or artists may be highly skilled in their particular area, but this does not mean that they are highly intelligent. We frequently overestimate the talented person's general intelligence, while, in fact, his specialty often limits his experience and knowledge about other fields of endeavor. Unusual accomplishments are generally due to some special capacity the person has, such as a color sense, physical coordination, and so on, which may be unrelated to intelligence.

Use the Polygraph When Advisable

Many restaurant managers say: "Why spend all this time and effort checking into people's backgrounds. We can give them a polygraph test and learn the whole story in a matter of an hour or two with much less trouble." In theory, the lie detector used at the point of employment might seem to be a logical answer to screening job applicants. Certainly many companies use it today, and may feel it is effective. But three states have banned the polygraph at the point of employment, and twelve states have statutes restricting its use in personnel work. The polygraph has extremely useful applications in business, particularly as a tool for investigating crime and for probing the details of employee dishonesty after a crime has been uncovered. But used at the point of employment, it raises some serious questions.

Through the efforts of the American Polygraph Association to establish a code of ethics and to police its members, the standards of professionalism in this field have risen steadily. Members of the A.P.A. must be college graduates, have matriculated in a polygraph school, and have served a six-month internship, among other requirements. While there are many extremely talented, well-trained, knowledgeable polygraph operators of the highest personal integrity, despite the men of achievement in the field, there are still other operators who are poorly trained, inexperienced, and lacking in psychological understanding who may be incapable of running reliable tests. The problem here is in locating the true professional and in avoiding the incompetent practitioner.

While the legal status of the polygraph is currently in a state of flux, as of this writing, only 16 states have enacted laws requiring polygraph operators to be licensed. In the remaining 34 states, you do not need to have a license to operate a polygraph; there are no educational requirements. All you need is the money to buy a machine and a good sales pitch. Therefore, as one precaution, any company that is considering using polygraph tests should assure itself that the practitioner has been accepted for membership in the A.P.A.

In addition to the question of a lack of professional standards, many factors can cause a wrong diagnosis, and only the qualified operator has the training and experience to make an expert decision. Any really qualified polygraph operator will tell you that an inaccurate polygraph test can be caused by illness, pain, coughing spells, mental or physical fatigue, heart conditions, hay fever, asthma, tranquilizing drugs, and so on. Even how the examiner acts toward the subject before the test can have an effect on the results. These are only a few of the many problems encountered.

The really qualified examiner can spot these problems, and he will tell you that he cannot get a reliable reading of the subject. Also, a certain percentage of people who take the test neither pass nor fail it; they simply cannot be tested. Unfortunately, the less responsible operators tend to mislead the restaurateur and often claim specific results of innocence or guilt when, in actual fact, they are unable to make a professional determination based on the polygraph evidence. The genuine expert in polygraph work can spot variables and work around them or reschedule his test for another day, but the untrained operator may be ignorant of these factors and may therefore end up with a false reading.

Another drawback is that there is considerable evidence that using a polygraph for pre-employment testing can result in relationship problems between job applicants and the food service management that is considering them for employment. In fact, in many cases it adversely affects management's ability to build strong relationships of confidence with employees.

If, however, the company does choose to use the polygraph at the point of employment, then tests of employees should be made every six months or so, just as you would require semi-annual health tests. This insures that the employees are continuing to maintain a high standard of honesty. For example, one restaurant in Chicago had used the polygraph only at the time of employment. After the employees had passed the test and were hired, they were never given another polygraph examination. Recently, it was discovered that most of the employees who had passed the test when first employed were now stealing from the restaurant on a large scale. The tested staff members apparently felt free to steal because they believed the test had proven them honest in the eyes of management.

Granted that the polygraph could be effective in screening if periodic tests were given to employees, but this is costly, time-consuming, and tends to set up a threatening work environment between management and staff. A nonthreatening work relationship is vital to reducing internal theft losses. Only in this atmosphere can employees grow, develop, and mature. The use of the polygraph may tend to destroy such a relationship. While it should be used in criminal investigations, it is a questionable substitute for the usual interviewing and screening methods used at the point of employment.

Apply These Steps Systematically

Understanding these fundamentals of personnel screening is only the first step. You have to make them work. A sound approach to personnel selection requires self-discipline. You must force yourself to study each person you consider hiring even more closely than before. At first, it will be difficult, tiresome, and tedious. Then one day it will all come together, and the next thing you know you will have developed an intuitive professional technique of personnel selection. For now, you may have to do it one step at a time, thinking out the process as you go along; but soon it will become automatic for you.

Remember that screening employees is one of the most important jobs in the entire company. Of course, you will have some failures, even if you follow all of the suggestions outlined in this section. But don't let the failures discourage you. Everyone has failures, at times, whenever judgment is involved. Your goal should be to make a better-than-average percentage of right decisions. So when you do make an error and one of your carefully screened people turns out to be dishonest, don't let this discourage you. Your objective is to do a professional hiring job, and you improve your average by applying a scientific and systematic approach to screening personnel applicants.

In this chapter you have all the tools you need to do an effective professional selection job. But like any tools, they require some actual practice and experience before you become skilled at using them. However, keep in mind that they have been proven remarkably effective in many food operations. Remember: The personnel decision is the ultimate method of controlling internal thefts.

In Summary

Summing up the main steps you should take to develop a comprehensive screening program that will enable you to hire the right people:

1. Don't judge an applicant by surface impressions. Glibness, a smooth appearance, and neat writing can't be substitutes for real character and ability.
2. Search for the person's true inner qualities such as integrity, tact, maturity, persistence.
3. Check the entire background, including all references (in person or by phone), some peers or associates, past jobs, employment gaps, adjustment in family, financial pressures, any possible police record. Don't expect anyone to reform.
4. Ask probing questions during the interview; watch for giveaway gestures.

5. Study the job experience on the application form carefully, and make sure the applicant fills out a bonding form.

6. Try to hire people of above average intelligence.

7. Be on guard for the fearless psychotic.

8. If you must use a polygraph, make sure it's in the hands of an expert.

3

Spotting the
High-Risk Employee

A 36-year-old restaurant chain operations vice president has been a loyal employee for nine years and is considered a model executive. Joe is a devoted family man, married with two children. He is a skillful administrator and completely trusted. He has worked his way through the ranks, staring as a trainee in one of the restaurants.

One day management stumbles onto the apparent fact that its model executive has been systematically embezzling thousands of dollars from company funds. "I just can't believe it," is the reaction of the company's president. "Joe has been a hard worker and loyal employee if ever there was one. I never dreamed he would do anything like this. I never suspected a thing."

Of course the president didn't suspect. If he or anyone else had, Joe wouldn't have been able to fleece the company out of thousands of dollars.

Actually, Joe fits almost exactly into the mold of an "average dishonest employee" if there is such a thing. According to insurance company statistics, when an average dishonest employee is apprehended, he is 36 years old. He has worked in the company for the last nine years and has been stealing or embezzling for the past several years. He is living beyond his means and therefore needs an additional source of income—which comes from your profits. The dishonest employee is a male in 93% of the cases.

Studies indicate the following possible clues to watch for in a high-risk "model executive." Some of these traits may also apply to lower level employees who are prone to steal:

1. *Gambling.* A person who is a compulsive gambler loses money quickly and often needs extra funds to support not only his regular responsibilities, but also his habit. He is more willing to take a chance on horses, numbers, and restaurant merchandise.

2. *Serious Debts.* Employees being pressed by creditors are often tempted to dip into restaurant profits to meet their debts and satisfy the wolves yowling at their door.

3. *Heavy Drinking.* Heavy drinkers usually have serious psychological problems and pressures. They are frequently irresponsible in their work habits. Liquor quiets the nerves and clouds judgment, making stealing easier.

4. *Heavy or Irresponsible Borrowing.* A person who frequently borrows large amounts of money is often driven to steal from any available sources. He may borrow small amounts of money from fellow employees and then fail to repay them. You may spot some of his personal checks undated, postdated, or pastdated. Or he may ask others not to cash his checks for a while.

5. *Using Business Contacts Dishonestly.* People who make dishonest demands upon business contacts for "breaks" on such items as food or silverware, or for "gifts" are stealing indirectly. This can lead to more direct stealing. It can also hurt your restaurant's reputation.

6. *Associating with Unwholesome Individuals.* When people associate with dishonest or unwholesome people, they are likely to be influenced by their peers. They also have more access to helpmates in crime. Restaurant merchandise seems to find its way outside more easily when a friendly "fence" is waiting.

7. *Refusing to Take Vacations.* People who refuse to take vacations may feel that they can't risk having a substitute stumble over their financial manipulations.

8. *Overprotecting Work Records or Files.* A person who is reluctant to give up custody of records or files or who takes them home with him may be keeping incriminating facts and documents close to him. Even though he may be extremely neat and fastidious in his bookkeeping, his actions may signal that something is wrong.

9. *Overly-Eager-Beavering.* While conscientious employees are a plus, overly eager individuals who rush into work early and always leave late can sometimes be trying to create a hard-working, honest image to cover up their thefts.

10. *Tattle-Taling.* When an employee frequently turns in dishonest workers, he may actually be covering over his own guilt by shifting the blame to others.

11. *Loud and Offensive Bragging.* Braggarts often try to cover up feelings of inferiority and worthlessness by boasting about themselves and their exploits. It is sometimes wise to keep a watchful eye on people like this, for they may steal in order to live up to their boasts.

12. *Hostility or Criticism.* Like braggarts, people who are offensively hostile toward others or very critical of them are often trying to elevate themselves by downgrading others. These people may at times take their feelings of anger and/or worthlessness out in theft.

Warning Signals

Despite the best possible personnel screening measures, some dishonest employees may still be hired. Even though the employees you hire may all have a perfect record, circumstances in their lives may cause them to steal. Sometimes the restaurant itself may inadvertently trigger a theft. Elements in the working environment may put undue pressure or temptation on the employee. Obviously such pressures should be guarded against and eliminated whenever possible. But regardless of circumstance, management must protect the company's assets, and the best way to do this is to spot the high-risk employee before theft occurs.

Certain clues can warn an alert manager. Of course, these clues don't point unquestionably to a dishonest person, but they may suggest that an employee should be watched carefully. Here are some of the signals to watch for in spotting potential problem employees.

Compulsive Gambling

Compulsive gambling is the single most significant cause of employee theft. In a study of 1,000 embezzlers made by the U.S. Fidelity & Guaranty Co., gambling was listed as the cause of 23% of all theft incidents and was the most frequently cited theft motive.

A restaurant in Florida was suffering 5% inventory shortages, and the chain's management couldn't figure out why. It conducted a complete security survey and discovered that a porter was making a daily tour of the restaurant to pick up bets by employees. When the restaurant's manager heard about the survey, he shrugged it off and said, "Those 10-cent bets on numbers aren't going to lead any of our employees to steal from us."

But he was wrong. When the chain finally discharged the employees who were taking bets and warned the remaining employees that betting on company property and during work hours was cause for dismissal, the shortages dropped to 2% in six months and 1% in a year.

If you hear of employees at your restaurant placing bets on horses or numbers, you may decide to let it pass. However, you should realize that compulsive gambling is a disease. Studies indicate that there are some 6 million chronic gamblers in the U.S. Once gambling gets a foothold in your operation, it can spread through the restaurant. It can destroy employee morale and reduce productivity.

When an employee becomes a compulsive gambler, his personal philosophy may start to change. He tends to become "luck" oriented and develops a strong desire to "get something for nothing." Since he no longer believes in earning the things he wants, his productivity drops. He may become lazy and difficult to motivate.

Since gamblers ultimately lose, the compulsive gambler may run low on cash and therefore be compelled to steal from your restaurant. Certainly he is more inclined to do so than a nongambler. And while he may be unable to control his impulses, it is still your restaurant that pays the gambler's bills.

If some of your employees gamble, you should consider the following four steps to help eliminate it:

1. Make a definite statement to your employees of your own feelings against gambling and your company's opposition to it, if there is such a policy.
2. Bar all gambling on company property.
3. Go on record as encouraging strict enforcement of gambling laws in your community.
4. Take the time to explain to employees why gambling is harmful to them and to their restaurant.

Heavy Drinking

Any employee who is a heavy drinker—particularly if he drinks on the job—is an honesty risk. People can become tranquilized with only a few ounces of liquor. Some psychologists feel that liquor may be the most frequently used tranquilizer in the nation. An employee's judgment can become blurred in this state of temporary sedation. A man who is honest when sober may become a thief when drunk.

Restaurant managers generally recognize that a heavy drinker has problems. But they rarely see the threat he represents to the restaurant. Heavy drinking can be expensive. To preserve the appearance of being a social drinker (more desirable than being known as an "alcoholic"), the alcoholic may treat his friends to drinks. The amount of money spent on this may put him in great debt. Who is going to buy the next round of drinks? The restaurant perhaps.

Besides this, heavy drinking impairs judgment and cuts down on productivity. So even if an alcoholic does not steal outright, his drinking causes a loss in terms of both time and productivity.

Heavy or Irresponsible Borrowing

An employee may be under serious financial pressure because of excessive debts. Some people can't seem to handle their money responsibly. They don't budget or plan ahead, and they become victims of impulse buying and spending. A financially irresponsible person may soon be under severe pressure because of excessive debts. When creditors demand payment on bills, pressed employees often begin to feel very anxious. These are often the people who are most likely to dip into the restaurant till where the funds are easily available. If you notice that an employee is continually in debt and borrowing from others, you should keep a watchful eye on him.

Living beyond Means

One day a cashier in a Los Angeles restaurant showed up wearing a new $3,000 diamond-studded watch. Two months later she began sporting a fur coat. Not until a year later and thousands of dollars poorer did the manager of that restaurant discover she was stealing cash while working in the money room. If he originally had been alert to the possible telltale clues, he might have saved his restaurant a lot of money.

When an employee begins to acquire and brag about an overabundance of elegant jewelry, expensive clothing, luxury cars, or stereo sets, it may be a warning signal. Most employees can't afford to buy all these items on their salaries alone. But once they become accustomed to living beyond their means, it is hard for them to cut down. They have to struggle to keep up payments on their cars, televisions, and charge accounts.

What should you do if you suspect an employee is living far beyond his income? You'd have to consider the position he holds in the restaurant and his related theft potential. Determine whether he has access to cash and food items or just to food. See if he is in a position where he could embezzle from the company.

These questions can help you decide whether to launch an investigation into an employee's financial situation. But you also should remember that such probes—if they became known—could have a negative effect on honest employees in the company. So it is wise to undertake an investigation only in strict secrecy and only when you have strong reason to think the individual is a definite security risk.

If he is in a strategic position, an extensive investigation may be warranted. But if he holds a minor post and has little access to large sums of money and little chance to manipulate documents (signing phony invoices, altering amounts on checks, etc.), then it may not be worth spending a great deal of time or effort uncovering the true source of his income.

However, if you do decide to investigate—and if you haven't done so in your previous personnel screening—you might check records with the local police and in other cities where the employee has lived. You could also ask the local credit bureau to conduct a detailed credit investigation of the suspect. If feasible, you might contact the local bank and find out how often the employee is depositing money and how much. Is there a pattern to these deposits? Are they excessive?

It might also be a good idea to obtain all available details on the employee's spending—car payments, appliance payments, rent, or mortgage payments. Then compare his expenditures with his known income. Include income earned by any other members of his family who are employed. If the suspect's expenditures are much greater than his combined income from all sources, try to check discreetly to see if the suspect's family might have any additional means of income.

It's not a good idea to automatically accept an employee's explanation of how he happens to have extra money. You should investigate his story to determine all the facts. A tale of a sudden unexpected inheritance may be true, but the employee also may have invented a story to cover his stealing from the company. If you've completed a thorough investigation and can't find a reasonable explanation for the employee's sudden affluence, you ought to keep a careful eye on his activities and spot-check his work for irregularities.

Emotional Problems

An employee who is erratic in behavior or unpredictable in his reactions to job situations merits careful watching, since these may be signs of emotional upset. You should also be concerned about the employee who formerly appeared stable and well-adjusted but who quite suddenly seems to be nervous, worried, and overly-emotional. He may become sullen, withdrawn, or depressed. Perhaps he is even angry or hostile. Any type of severe personality fluctuation may indicate that a person is under serious psychological stress and needs special attention.

While the average restaurant manager is not a psychologist and is in no position to diagnose such problems, most managers can recognize signs of severe emotional upset. If an employee seems to have serious emotional problems, he may be a security risk to the restaurant.

Studies indicate that stealing is sometimes a reaction to a severe emotional crisis. Some people steal when they become depressed; some to "get even" with their bosses or with the company. Still others steal to gain status with peers. And others because they have guilt feelings and actually want to be caught and punished for these feelings.

When you notice an employee with a severe emotional problem, it might be wise for you to encourage him to seek professional help. If such action is not feasible, you certainly have an obligation to speak with him about the matter, especially since such an action may protect company assets.

Family Problems

A person with serious difficulties at home can wreak havoc on restaurant profits. Any number of problems may result in pressures that cause otherwise honest employees to steal.

A spouse may become ill or incapable of working. Medical bills may mount up along with pressures and worries. Even basically honest employees may steal as a last resort when they are faced with a desperate need for money.

Marital difficulties and problems can also lead to theft. Sudden new expenses may arise if a husband or a wife is deserted by a spouse. A divorced man who is obligated to support his former wife and children may find himself in an especially tight financial bind if he remarries. Financial adjustment for a recently divorced woman also may be difficult. Under new pressures and worries like these, such employees may feel compelled to steal cash or food items to supplement their incomes.

Often people outside the family feel guilty about suspecting someone in difficulty of stealing and prefer to admire their courage rather than question their honesty. While others can't help feeling sorry for them, it is nevertheless important to prevent them from committing dishonest act.

Violating Rules

You should also watch extra carefully any employee who rebels against general rules. Perhaps you notice him sneaking out of the restaurant before closing time, and having another employee stamp his time card for him. Or perhaps you spot him using an unauthorized exit to leave the restaurant. This failure to live by the rules may indicate a lack of responsibility that also manifests itself when this employee is handling cash or food items.

Chronic Lying

Some people lie when put under pressure. Others lie to protect someone else's feelings. Still others, when they are afraid of punishment. But a chronic liar tends to be a malad-justed person who lies compulsively for no apparent reason. Experience shows that a perpetual liar is a high theft risk and should be carefully watched.

Overly Attentive Employees

Perhaps you have an employee who always shows up for work a half hour or an hour early. He pitches in, straightens up the restaurant, and sets the tables long before other workers arrive. Such a person may be totally conscientious and an invaluable asset to your restaurant. But he may also be an honesty risk.

Some of the greatest thieves in the restaurant business have been superb actors. They try to get on the good side of the boss by doing personal favors. They may even cultivate you socially, invite you to their homes, or meet you at a bar outside the job. They may offer to handle menial tasks, run personal errands, or do any number of small favors to ingratiate themselves. This strategy can sometimes give them a smokescreen to hide behind.

You may find it hard to believe that a person who has done so much for you would ever steal from your restaurant. But a "trusted" person is the very one who can get away with large-scale thefts. We keep a careful eye on the person we don't trust, but we sometimes want to see only the good qualities of the trusted person. Instead, we should be alert to the fact that the overly attentive person in some cases may be stealing from us.

Long-Time Employees

Long term employees can sometimes be a more serious threat to restaurant profits than new ones, even if the new ones may steal more often. According to insurance company statistics, thefts of long-term employees involve much larger amounts of money than thefts of newer personnel. Since management is more likely to be suspicious of newer personnel, it tends to catch them stealing more often. But they have only recently started their theft activities. A long-term employee is likely to have built up a much more substantial theft total by the time he is caught.

Of course, most employees who have worked for a long period of time with a good work record are honest. However, this does not mean that you should close your eyes to any suspicions you may have about a previously "trusted" employee. After all, the long-term employee is more likely to know what the managers and restaurant check or do not check, how the restaurant systems and operations work, and what he can reasonably get away with. And if other workers are stealing, he'll know that too. His complete inside knowledge, plus the fact that most of his activities no longer arouse curiosity, make him a potentially great theft threat in terms of dollar losses.

PART 3
Preventing Theft

4

Employee Theft Methods

Try standing at your employee exit door one evening and watch the people leaving. Perhaps everything looks fine. There is no visible sign of stealing. Yet intuitively you get the feeling that at least one of your employees is stealing. But how? One night as you watch a cashier leaving the restaurant wearing a new fur-lined coat, you might start wondering if she paid for it out of your restaurant's profits. Another time you see Jimmy the storeroom man sneaking across the receiving dock toward his car during a break period when the dock is deserted. As he walks across the lot, you notice a big bulge under his jacket. As he gets into the car, you may wonder if that bulge is stolen merchandise.

If you've thought about these things, you're not alone. Restaurant managers across the country share these same doubts and concerns about some of their people. The big questions are: Where do you put your control emphasis, and how do you determine which areas need attention? Some of the answers come from knowing the main theft methods that your employees use. By looking carefully at these methods, you often can spot the loopholes that need to be tightened. Reviewing your control systems in the light of the actual theft methods is invaluable. Of course, just knowing the methods won't stop them, but it can pinpoint areas that need to be investigated and changes made.

Countermeasures are difficult to design unless you know how employees steal. No matter how smoothly things seem to be going, a manager should never get too smug about security. Internal theft is a constant danger that requires continuous monitoring to control. Knowledge of the methods and what they mean gives you a valuable edge over your restaurant's invisible opponents.

Apprehending a dishonest employee serves little purpose if nothing is done to change the conditions which led to the dishonesty. Each case should be carefully reviewed and the prime causes determined. Weaknesses in control systems and procedures, a breakdown in supervision, or whatever has permitted a particular theft method to flourish should be identified and remedied. Each case can be an important lesson to help you improve your security.

Security experts estimate that there are literally thousands of methods by which employees can steal. But the techniques don't vary greatly. Many are simply variations of basic technique categories. These categories tend to involve cash register thefts, food supply thefts, collusive thefts, embezzlement, and fraud.

How Employees Discover the Methods

Employees have to discover possible theft methods before they can implement them. Usually these discoveries relate to weaknesses in restaurant controls. Employees may even stumble across possible theft methods quite by accident. For example, an employee may discover a $5 bill behind the cash register drawer and may reason that the register has been short $5 for quite a while. Since the manager hasn't indicated anything is missing, the employee may feel that either management is careless or it doesn't consider the loss important.

So the employee may decide to put his theory to the test. When he is on the cash register the next day, he withholds $5. But he keeps the $5 bill available so that he could claim it fell behind the wastebasket if anyone's suspicions are aroused. In many restaurants a small shortage is not noticed. When the employee sees that management once again doesn't miss the money, he knows he has found a theft method that works.

Employees can also learn theft methods from their peers. All too often, fellow employees admire someone who can beat the system. They regard successful stealing as an achievement. Theft contamination may spread, and the thieves may become heroes to their fellow workers. Employees may even discuss theft methods as casually as they discuss yesterday's shopping expedition or last night's movie.

Finally, when a dishonest employee observes loopholes in a restaurant's control systems or in its supervision, he'll try to beat the system. He will seek the cooperation of other employees in his efforts, and he will learn by observing other dishonest workers. If he happens to have a dishonest supervisor, the contamination will spread even faster.

Once we know how employees steal, we are in a better position to cope with theft and prevent it. Let's explore some of the main theft techniques.

Switching Checks

A form of internal theft in which the restaurant doesn't lose money directly but which can arouse the antagonism of the customers if discovered involves the switching of checks. This is more prevalent in dinner houses where the waiter collects the money from the table and brings it to the open cash register for change than in other types of operations.

Suppose, for example, that there are two parties in the restaurant—one with a $40 check and the other with a $50 check. The waiter first presents the $50 check to the $40 table and keeps the $40 check. If the party pays the $50 plus tip, he turns in only $40 and pockets $10. Then he presents the same $50 correct check to the second party.

If the first party should notice the "mistake," the waiter merely apologizes for his error and presents the correct $40 check. If the first party signs the check or pays by credit card, the scheme is usually thwarted. But the same waiter may try again later, since nobody can really prove that he tried to steal.

Besides costing a restaurant future business from irritated customers and damaging its reputation, such methods can lead to wider employee thefts throughout the restaurant. Once the word gets around that a restaurant is vulnerable up front, theft may spread to other sections of the restaurant like a contagious disease.

How the Items "Sneak Out"

One of the favorite employee theft routes is the back door. Cartons of foodstuffs or supplies can be pushed near a rear door and tossed into an employee's car outside when nobody is looking. Small items can be slipped under a door and later picked up outside.

In one Indiana restaurant where the rear door was always locked, employees complained of poor ventilation and asked the manager to leave the back door open. Naïve as it may seem, he agreed. One of the receiving workers, saying he needed fresh air, would make quick frequent trips outside carrying a carton of items with him each time he left. He would put the cartons in his car, which he always kept parked near the receiving door. Over a period of nine months, he managed to haul away some $2,000 worth of goods.

The most common form of back door theft, however, is to simply toss items out the door and have someone else come along later and pick them up. "The theft of raw food products out my back door is the worst single problem I encounter in my restaurants," said the operations vice president of one Florida-based chain. "There are so many variations of this that it's hard to keep up with them all."

When the back door is unavailable, there are many other routes open to employees. Steaks can be wrapped in aluminum foil and go out with the trash or laundry to be picked up later. Wine bottles can be concealed in overcoats and smuggled out. Meats and canned goods can be dropped out of windows to be retrieved by friends. Food, candy, liquor, cigarettes, table linens, and dishes can be hidden in handbags, briefcases, and paper-wrapped packages, under coats or in the pockets of outer garments and taken home by the employee. Silverware can be put in a pocket and carried out. Or—particularly in a fast food operation—an employee can stuff a few burgers in his pocket, walk outside for a minute, and slip the burgers to his buddy in the parking lot.

In one Michigan restaurant an employee was able to carry steaks out the door a few evenings every week upon leaving work. He concealed them under his hat, and nobody bothered to ask him to take his hat off. This went on for a year until the manager happened to notice a streak of juice coming from his hat and running down his cheek one night.

Storage Area Thefts

The storage area can be a source of tremendously high thefts—especially late at night when the restaurant is not as heavily supervised as at other times. Since internal theft becomes a greater threat from these areas at times when there are fewer people around, the manager should be especially careful and alert during these periods. Employees may clip the restaurant for thousands of dollars worth of storage area merchandise.

In the case of one New Orleans restaurant, storeroom personnel carted out steaks in boxes and loaded their trunks with foodstuffs every night. One man actually pulled up in a rental truck and loaded it to capacity.

In another, a security specialist hired to investigate losses found that the night crew had worked together to steal some $14,000 worth of goods during a 2 year period. The crew had found a loophole in the restaurant's security system. Every night a central alarm system preventing the use of unauthorized entrances and exits was turned off for 15 minutes. That period was sufficient for the night crew to pass in and out several times carrying armloads of food items.

Vendor Kickbacks

When employees work together to steal from your restaurant, it is a sad, costly situation. But employee collusion with an outsider is even more dangerous and can result in bigger losses. It may involve a chain buyer's ordering a certain quantity or quality of items, but having fewer or poorer quality items actually delivered to your restaurant. Here's how it's done.

Let's say that the buyer orders 250 pounds of prime beef ribs. The meat producer delivers ribs of beef, but not prime. And he delivers 200 pounds intead of the 250 that were ordered. If your receiving clerk is in collusion with the meat supplier, he will confirm that the quantity and quality of the meat received is correct. The receiving clerk and the buyer will then get a share of the money stolen—or a kickback.

The kickback is one of the worst forms of theft collusion. Many restaurant firms close their eyes to vendor kickbacks and pretend that they have no way to prevent it. But kickbacks are more prevalent than many people would like to admit.

Vendor collusion in deliveries occurs frequently at restaurants in any number of ways. Working with a dishonest employee, a dishonest vendor's representative can inflate the invoice by making a deliberate error in multiplying price extensions or in totaling the bill. If not discovered, he can then split the overpayment with the employee.

A deliveryman can deliver only two-thirds of a promised meat order to a restaurant and sell the balance to another restaurant, splitting the difference with the dishonest employee. The employee simply signs for meat that is never really unloaded from the delivery truck.

Variations of vendor collusion at restaurants include: delivering the correct number of items and then removing some of them under the guise of returning unsatisfactory merchandise; or removing foodsuffs that are stale and shorting the restaurant on the credit due for such returns.

At the management level, buyers can be corrupted by dishonest suppliers who sell second-grade products at first-grade prices and offer kickbacks in return. Because of normal variations in quality, such kickbacks are sometimes difficult to detect. In some cases the buyer himself takes the responsibility for inspecting incoming items. But in other cases he forces the receiving clerk to accept substandard perishables to satisfy the supplier who is giving him monthly kickbacks.

Rigging invoices is another buying office fraud method. The buyer approves an inflated invoice and gets a kickback from the supplier on the overpayment.

In one flagrant example of headquarters fraud, the executives of a major restaurant chain became suspicious that its buyers and middle management were receiving substantial kickbacks from suppliers. The word was that the buyers might be receiving their kickbacks on the form of government bonds. So the chain's president hired a team of investigators and gave them a list of all his buyers, as well as their secretaries, wives, and family members. The investigators spent weeks searching the public records for people's names and addresses who had been assigned such bonds. These efforts paid off, however, when the investigators uncovered the names of seven company executives who had received a total of over $200,000 in kickbacks from suppliers.

Embezzlement

Embezzlement involves the fraudulent appropriation of cash, checks, or securities which have been entrusted to an employee's care. The two most vulnerable areas are the cashier's office and the accounting department where checks are disbursed.

Check forgery is the most common form of embezzlement found in a company. Employees have used more than 800 different ways of defrauding their companies with bank checks, according to W. E. Rose, an authority on crimes involving bank clerks. For example, an employee in the accounting department may make out a duplicate salary check in his own name. He then watches for the original cancelled check, takes it out of the incoming mail from the bank, and destroys it. He tries to conceal his actions and balance the accounts by raising the amount on several legitimate cancelled checks.

Among other methods of check disbursement thefts are: intercepting a check payable to the company and forging the company's name; increasing the face amount of a check or changing the name of the payee; paying an invoice twice and appropriating the second check; and simply stealing a check that has been made payable to cash.

Thefts committed by bookkeepers or cashiers are especially costly because they aren't usually discovered until great damage already has been done, and because the bookkeeping and cashier's offices provide opportunities for a great diversity of fraud. Thus embezzlement and fraud techniques might also include: delaying or shorting bank deposits; establishing a dummy resource firm so that checks paid by the restaurant on the dummy invoices can be cashed; padding the payroll by adding fictitious names; cashing unclaimed wage checks; overloading expense accounts; inserting fictitious ledger sheets; stealing incoming payments; and making false bookkeeping entries.

Manipulating Computers

Computers can be very efficient for restaurant chains with big payrolls; however, they also are vulnerable to clever thieves in the company. In one chain headquartered in the Midwest, an assistant manager was studying computer programming at night in a local school. After several months of such study, he managed to get into the computer room on the second floor when nobody was there. In 20 minutes he manipulated the program tape as he had been taught and "tipped" the computer. He gave himself a neat weekly raise that upped his salary from $200 to $300 on the tape that punched out computer-written bank checks. It was more than a year before the auditors, trying to find a discrepancy in payout figures, uncovered the culprit. By that time he had embezzled about $6,000 from the firm.

Computer thefts of this type at both the restaurant and headquarters level are likely to become more frequent as the industry becomes more sophisticated and computerized. As computer equipment becomes more complex and less understandable to management, more serious crimes relating to manipulation of computer records are likely. Theoretically, thieves could wipe out an entire chain by using the company's own computer programs to embezzle millions of dollars before the company could discover what had happened.

Discovering the "Why's"

Harry Jones, a restaurant manager in Sacramento, Calif., caught a cashier giving free meals to his friends. When the manager discovered what was happening, he discharged the cashier on the spot. It was the fifth time in the last seven months that Harry had to get rid of a cashier for being so accommodating to friends.

Roger Thomson, a restaurant manager in San Diego, was running into the same kind of problem on a different level. The other night he received a phone call from the police at 1 A.M. that his cook had been caught stealing items from the storeroom. Roger promptly fired the cook and started looking for a new one. Interestingly enough, just a few months earlier Roger had fired his dishwasher when he was found looting the deep freezer.

One way of looking at these two situations is that Harry and Roger were staying well ahead of employee theft at their restaurants. After all, they had tackled the theft problem head-on by discharging numerous employees and were really making inroads into a more secure operation. Right? Wrong! Unfortunately, neither man had taken the time to discover *why* these thefts occurred and *why* they were repeated. Nothing had really been solved.

Their mistake was to approach the theft situation in their restaurants as if each individual incident was a problem in and of itself. Instead, they should have taken all of the incidents together as a warning signal that certain unidentified and more basic problems existed in their operations—problems that encouraged dishonety. Instead, the approaches they had chosen made it impossible for them to take intelligent, corrective action.

Let's suppose that you went out to your garage and found that your car wouldn't start. That would be a problem. But would your real problem be the fact that your car wouldn't start, or would it be that you ran out of gas or that your battery went dead? You would correct the condition by filling the gas tank or recharging the battery. The point is that you should treat the *cause* not the *symptom*.

What does this mean to Harry and all restaurant managers faced with repeated theft incidents? It means that you must analyze each dishonest employee case to uncover the underlying causes of the situation and to develop effective countermeasures to prevent such thefts from recurring. Intensive analysis can reveal physical limitations and loopholes in control systems or unsatisfactory supervisory performance. It can also indicate specific weaknesses such as the lack of physical barriers and inadequate locks. It can reveal which controls are ineffective or missing entirely, and which management practices and employee attitudes need changing. Ironically, the greatest value achieved from apprehending a dishonest employee may not be removing a thief from your operation, but rather learning about proper security enforcement of your restaurant.

Trial and error is sometimes the only way to discover the real causes of the theft problem. Normally, there are several possible causes for any given theft situation. At first glance these numerous combinations might look like a tangled mess. But by analyzing the situation step by step in systematic fashion, you will often discover that the number of possible causes can be reduced to a limited number of possibilities. These can be feasibly examined and tested with a relatively small amount of time and effort.

Your main objective is to separate the whole into its component parts. It's like taking apart a clock to see what makes it tick. You separate each spring and gear, laying them out on the table. Then you examine each part for weaknesses with a magnifying glass. You search for missing units, cogs that are bent, or wheels that are warped. Are any of the cogs or wheels missing? Is the mainspring broken? Are the parts covered with grease and dirt from misuse? Is the unit suffering from neglect? In this same manner you can reduce a complex theft situation to workable size through analysis.

But how can you undertake analysis without an actual theft apprehension? If you know that heavy shortages exist but that a suspect has not yet been identified, first check each element in the procedural control system. After this, check the adequacy of the enforcement procedures. Then study the physical layout at the back of the house, front of the house, and cash registers.

It is always easier to analyze the situation when you have a suspect in an actual case. This at least gives you a starting point for probing the real causes of your losses. If you discover a dishonest employee in a restaurant who shows extreme shortages, this brings the problem into greater focus.

Committee Review

Every restaurant should have a program requiring the systematic review of any dishonest employee case within a reasonable period after the employee is caught. It is important to undertake a review while all the facts are still fresh in the minds of the people who investigated it. Who conducted the interrogation? Who was involved? Any internal control problems should be corrected as soon as possible before they snowball. A dishonest employee case often is like a creak in the dam of the restaurant's security; the sooner it is repaired, the less likely it is that stealing will grow to major proportions.

While there is a tendency for restaurateurs to close their eyes to dishonest practices, this only allows further stealing to continue. A practical type of systematic program that a restaurant company might want to start could be organized along these lines:

1. Launch a program to gain maximum insight into every theft case that occurs by organizing a case analysis committee. Its role should be to analyze every case, to spot the causes to the theft, and to identify the operating weaknesses which have allowed the theft to occur. Try to include two or three top management people as permanent committee members. These might be the restaurant manager, controller, personnel director, and security director.

2. Set a specific day and time for periodic review of any theft cases that have occurred. Give the committee all the known facts in the case beforehand so they are prepared to discuss causes and possible countermeasures.

3. Start the monthly meeting by having the committee convener read a summary of the case to refresh the minds of the members and to provide any further details. Be sure that all committee members clearly have the facts relating to the incident. Encourage them to ask questions to make sure they fully understand the case. They should be familiar with these specifics:

   a. The method of theft.
   b. The length of time covered by the thefts and their frequency.
   c. The kind of items stolen.
   d. The extent of admitted thefts.
   e. Whether or not there were accomplices.
   f. Any other details; e.g., what might have triggered the thefts, how many people were involved, etc.

4. Once all the facts are out on the table, you can throw the case open for discussion. Committee members should focus on one major question: How can such thefts be prevented in the future? In essence, who was the dishonest employee? How carefully was he screened before he was hired? Were his references checked? If so, were there any negative factors which should have made the restaurant more cautious in hiring him? Was his job performance reviewed recently by his supervisor? What were the findings? How did the supervisor feel about him as a worker and as a person? Did he ever have any doubts about his honesty? Had he reported his suspicions to anyone? What went wrong with the control systems and procedures? Why did this case occur? What can management learn from it?

5. If the committee has explored the entire problem in a logical fashion, it should reach some important decisions

for improving restaurant operations, supervision, security or control systems, and procedures. Once the committee decides what action to take, corrective measures should be assigned to those responsible. If the problem is complex and requires an approach from several angles, it may be advisable to establish a timetable for action. You might also decide to have intermediate reports on the progress being made to correct the underlying causes of the theft problem. Then you would follow up to see that your plan or corrective action is being carried out as intended.

If properly analyzed, every dishonest employee case can disclose important information to management: facts that can improve internal controls and supervision, management's relationship with its employees, problems of employee attitudes and morale. This can all be done quickly and efficiently—and with handsome results in curbing the sources and causes of future potential internal thefts.

5

Controls of the
Supply Function

To minimize pilferage, control of all major restaurant activities from back to front of the house is a must. This includes purchasing, receiving, storing, issuing, and production control—known as the *supply function.*

Keep careful track of all items from the time they are received through each step until the invoices are paid. This discourages theft along the "pipeline." Keeping strict controls over these areas has a built-in psychological effect that may also help to prevent employee dishonesty.

Purchasing

Effective controls must start with purchasing. This should be done by competitive bid. To accomplish this, you must have a set of detailed purchase specifications which you should give to your suppliers. You should also be sure that the items and quantities to be bought are recorded on a competitive want list so you will be able to compile and compare the various price quotations. This will also minimize the possibility of kickbacks.

The severity of the kickback problem has been disputed among members of the industry for years. Certainly, collusion between food buyers and suppliers does exist. Illegal "deals" may result in accepting inferior grade products at premium prices or approving invoices for goods that were never received.

During his first day on the job, a new food buyer for a Chicago restaurant was visited by the vice president of a meat supply house. The man came to offer his congratulations to the food buyer, as well as his help and services. On his way out of the office, he casually left an envelope on the food buyer's desk—which the food buyer discovered several hours later—containing two new $100 bills.

Seeing the envelope and guessing who had left it, the food buyer immediately telephoned the vice president and requested that a messenger be sent to pick up the envelope. Fortunately for the restaurant, their food buyer was honest. Had he not been, the restaurant could have suffered considerable losses.

What can you do when a buyer accepts payoffs from a purveyor for dealing exclusively with him or pays higher prices to one purveyor? Your best control on this is to investigate market prices yourself to make sure you are getting the best deals and that your buyer is working in your best interests. By the time you discover a buyer who is getting payoffs from a purveyor, you may already have suffered severe losses. But at least you can prevent this from happening in the future. And your investigation of the market may even uncover certain low-priced deals that your most honest buyer may have overlooked. But remember: The lowest priced merchandise is not necessarily the best buy.

Receiving

In most restaurants, receiving is not given the importance that it should be. Some of the reasons for this are:

1. The receiving personnel often lack specific responsibilities or training for the job.

2. Low wage rates result in mediocre competence among receiving personnel.

3. Frequent turnover in the receiving area means that restaurants lose whatever training has been accomplished and must start over again.

There are often few if any checks on incoming merchandise. Items may be short on quantity, quality, or both. Therefore, it is especially important to check all items to be sure you are getting exactly what you have requested and are paying for. Failure to do so offers opportunities for a variety of people—truck drivers, purveyors, or receiving personnel themselves—to steal.

One way to check the items being received is through the use of the buyer's specification and want lists. These lists include the quantity or weight, grade, and quality of major items, so incoming merchandise can be checked accurately. Your specifications should tell you everything possible about your merchandise, including such details as trim, whether bone in or out, size, grade, etc.

Deficiencies in receiving must be recorded immediately upon receipt of merchandise on a credit memo (p. 68). This is a major device for enforcing proper receiving procedures. Credit memos should be prepared in duplicate, so that they won't be ignored at the end of the month and so that accounting can deduct the value of defective merchandise from the end-of-the-month statement. Any deficiency (short weights, other shortages, insufficient quality, back orders, errors in price, errors in extention, and deposit returns) should be recorded on these forms. They can then be summarized and evaluated in order to measure effective receiving procedures.

Installing and using scales is one of the quickest and easiest ways of making certain that you are not being shorted on meats and other bulk items. Printing devices attached to scales can verify billed quantities, provided that the items on the invoice are unwrapped and individually weighed, as they should be.

One restaurant that bought fresh chickens from Arkansas received them in ice packs with a description of their weights

WILLIAM ALLEN & CO., N.Y. STOCK FORM 7114

REQUEST FOR CREDIT MEMO.

N? 802

DATE _____

TO _____

GENTLEMEN:

Please send us Credit Memo for the following:

YOUR INVOICE NO. _____

REASON:

BY _____

on the box. When they were actually unpacked and weighed without the ice, however, they were found to be several pounds under what they were marked as.

In the area of portion control meats, checking weights and quantities is especially important. Many restaurants will be deficient in the number, weight, or grade of meat. One restaurateur I know of ordered 6-ounce chopped steak patties for his operation, which were delivered to him in 10-pound boxes. It took over a year for the operator to realize that 6-ounce patties do not go evently into 10-pound boxes. He was being shorted 4 ounces on each box over a period of a year.

Getting incorrect merchandise happens in areas of the restaurant operation besides just the kitchen itself. One operator ordered 60 cases of blended whiskey in quart bottles at an extremely favorable price from a dealer. When the cases came into the warehouse, they were counted and found to be correct in number. But when the owner himself checked them over, he discovered that the dealer had sent fifths, not quarts. While this may have been an accident—and many mistakes are— nevertheless, such errors deplete profits.

Another control crucial to receiving is checking invoices. Prices are often accidentally or intentionally in error, so it is vitally important to make sure that they are as quoted. Extensions and additions should be checked as well, even if these tasks require additional manpower.

Most well-run establishments have full-time auditing departments to check invoices. However, the owner of one small restaurant felt he couldn't afford a full-time person. Nevertheless, he decided to hire a part-time person who would do nothing but check the mathematics of his invoices to see if there would be any difference in his figures. The employee worked four hours a day, five days a week, at $2.25 an hour. After invoices were checked for six months, the restaurant received back four times the amount it was paying the part-time employee!

More and more restaurants are turning to another alternative to control receiving: making two or more people responsible for the receiving. Some restaurants still assign just one person—usually the cook—to do this job. However, many operations are asking their managers, assistant managers, or manager trainees to check in the merchandise as well. Having both management and accounting personnel assist with the receiving provides another safeguard against theft.

Many small restaurants set up their own standards for receiving. This is fine, provided that whoever receives the merchandise is competent to know what he is supposed to be getting. This is particularly true in our business, where perishables must be fresh and of good quality. Too many restaurants are lax about incoming merchandise and accept almost anything that comes in. This is inexcusable, in view of the fact that merchandise represents cash in another form.

Sometimes this happens because restaurant personnel are just too lazy to report deficiencies or irregularities in receiving. One Texas restaurant regularly bought prime ribs of beef from a New York meat vendor. As a precautionary measure, the new manager decided to conduct a spot check on the receiving area.

The manager found an invoice for 365 pounds of prime ribs at the regular price. But when he opened the package and weighed the merchandise, he found only 325 pounds of prime ribs and 40 pounds of bones!

Apparently the food buyer was aware of the situation—which had been occurring for some time—and had permitted it to continue. So the manager showed the buyer what this carelessness had cost the restaurant in terms of profits and gave him a severe warning not to let it happen again.

Another important rule to remember for receiving control is to keep the back door locked at all times. Self-locking devices are available to insure that this is done. No one should be permitted to enter or exit without the manager's knowledge, consent, and/or presence. Any unauthorized personnel should be kept out of the back-of-the-house area.

One small Kentucky restaurant allowed milk drivers to enter through the back way unsupervised in order to put the milk they delivered directly into the dairy refrigerators. While the milk drivers did this as a favor, they also continuously removed some swiss cheese and eggs on their way out. Had the back door been more carefully supervised, this could never have occurred.

Among the elements of a good receiving system are:

1. Record all shipments as soon as they come in the back door of your restaurant.
2. Be sure that for every shipment received and put into stock, an invoice is charged within the same accounting period, in order to avoid differences in inventory reconciliation.
3. Guarantee that there will be no duplicate payment of the invoice, and seek quick payment to get discounts.
4. Take end-of-month inventories and reconcile them.
5. Provide records that enable auditors to check the validity of paid invoices, such as printed weight verification.

Procedural controls are particularly important to prevent irregularities in receiving process or manipulation of purchase journals and accounts payable records. Dishonest employees may manipulate and falsify records in order to convert food into cash. You can safeguard your receiving area from such incidents by insisting on good supervision, adequate physical protection, and sensible control systems and procedures. A little effort in establishing effective controls can go a long way in avoiding the disastrous shortages that many restaurants suffer.

Storing and Issuing

All incoming shipments should be stored or refrigerated promptly. Canned and staple goods should be price-marked. This makes the costing of issuing records easier. High-cost items such as steaks should be entered in a perpetual inventory record. This record, if properly maintained by a management staff member, should help you to reconcile daily items issued to the kitchen with those reported as sold. If there are differences between these two figures, you should investigate them immediately and determine their cause. A simple inventory control form on which to compare the quantities consumed with those shown on guest checks can simplify this procedure.

Depending on the physical circumstances, merchandise can be effectively controlled by keeping it in locked or attended storage areas. In one Virginia restaurant, two pantry women had access to an unlocked storeroom. Every few days they removed several cans of tunafish and salmon and a two-pound bag of coffee in their handbags. Over a period of six months, this reduced restaurant profits by several percentage points. This is the kind of unnecessary loss that can be avoided with a minimum of time and effort.

Such merchandise should be made available to kitchen employees only if they have a written requisition. These requisitions become issuing records, which are one element of a periodical inventory reconciliation (opening inventory + purchases − recorded issues = expected closing inventory). You can then use them to compare expected inventory with the actual physical inventory count to determine possible storeroom shortages.

Production Control

It is very important that you as a restaurant owner or manager determine the quantities of major entree items. These quantities can then be requisitioned from a locked storage area and be made available to the head cook or production supervisor to be prepared according to recipe and/or portion size standards. At the end of each meal period, unsold entrees should be recorded and deducted from the issued quantities. The difference between these two figures, known as "quantities consumed," should be compared with the number of the same items reported on guest checks. This will discourage theft by employees who take such items home.

However, if shortages recur, frequent, unannounced inventories are one way of discouraging thievery. Items should be traced through the restaurant from the time they enter the receiving room. Thus if you normally receive 150 pounds of beef round but have received only 100 pounds on a particular day, the cook should report that he is short 50 pounds. If you have traced this item through the processing line, you can clearly hold the receiving clerk responsible for the apparent shortage.

Inventory Systems

If you make it a point to personally walk through all areas of your restaurant a few times a day, you will help discourage potential thieves. An employee who thinks you might suddently appear or make a surprise inspection is apt to think twice before trying to swipe an item. But you can't depend on being in all places at all times and need to build in systematic protections.

This means a constant awareness of all the goods you have on hand. You should have a separate stock card for high-cost items and keep it in an inventory book. Initial entries indicate the date received, quantity, and price. As these goods are taken from stock, they are posted on the same stock cards. Thus you always know what should be in your stockrooms. By comparing your inventory records with your actual stock, you can tell if items have disappeared without a requisition and can follow up with an investigation.

Even this system however, may be too complex for smaller restaurants. You may not want to keep an individual card for too many items; nevertheless, you should still use some version of this system. Bear in mind that the object of inventory records is to prevent any items from leaving the stockroom without authorization. Nobody should be authorized to put out food without a written order to account for it.

But there are certain types of employee thefts that won't show up in your inventory systems for quite awhile. One such instance occurs when employees help themselves to your food. This is usually more of a nuisance than a major loss, although it shouldn't be permitted to continue. Far more serious is a cook who sells food directly to a dishwasher at a discounted price. This is something you must be alert to, and once you spot it, you must take immediate action—a warning or possibly even dismissal—against the offenders. This is one way to dissuade other employees from this practice.

Commissaries

If you have a commissary, it can be one of the most vulnerable areas to heavy internal theft losses. To protect yourself against this threat, you need controls and cross-checks at each point where food changes hands. Starting with purchasing, these controls parallel the movement of food throughout the entire handling process from receiving to storage, requisitioning, preparation, and distribution.

Employees are draining too many commissaries of food and profits. The principle is the same at those commissaries which are designed to operate at a break-even point while each individual restaurant makes the profit. Employee theft at such commissaries creates a net loss at the commissary level and constitutes a profit drain on the whole company.

You can avoid these dangers by installing the suggested controls. Perhaps you'll be pleasantly surprised and find that your commissary can be operated profitably even when you intend to just break even!

One final rule to keep in mind in all food operations to avoid unnecessary risks: Separate the three main restaurant control functions—cash handling, accounting, and inventory control. By having these areas handled by different people, you will limit your potential losses and increase the chances of discovering problems and inconsistencies more quickly.

6

Safeguarding the Bar

Bill, the always smiling beer-bellied bartender, loved to pour drinks for his fellow employees, friends, relatives, and just about anyone else. The catch was that many of these drinks were on the house. Bill craved the power and popularity that seemed to go with these freebies. But after a while the restaurant began to become concerned about this practice—especially when it led to heavy inventory shortages in liquor. After all, the bar is a business, not a popularity contest.

Not surprisingly, employee pilferage or the dispensing of free or additional drinks (really forms of theft) are probably more prevalent at the bar than anywhere else in the restaurant. Since many restaurants derive as much as 25% to 40% of their volume from alcoholic beverages, and since liquor has a considerably higher profit margin and greater loss potential than food, this is a problem that merits close examination.

The bar is a tempting target. Often a bartender like Bill operates with almost no supervision. Furthermore, all that valuable liquor in one place often creates more of a temptation than an employee can resist. There's also sometimes a feeling that a little extra liquor won't be missed, that management doesn't care, or that employees are entitled to liquor as part of the rewards of their job.

In terms of actual stealing at the bar, there are three main methods by which bartenders cheat the management: 1) pocketing cash, 2) liquor pilferage and related irregularities, and 3) bringing in outside merchandise.

Pocketing Cash

Bartenders use a number of methods to pocket money given to him by the customer. One way is to pour the customer his drink and avoid ringing up the sale. This way the sale is never registered and the bartender can feel relatively safe that his crime will go undetected. Or he can underring the price of the drink, charge the customer the correct price, and pocket the difference.

In both these cases, bartenders sometimes leave the money in the register until closing to avoid risking detection. Then, if he has access to the day's sales total, he can postpone pocketing the money until the end of the shift, count the cash in the register, and remove any money in excess of the day's readings.

One way to discourage this is to forbid the bartender access to the cash register reading. If the bartender has no way of finding out what the day's sales amount to, it will be much more difficult for him to postpone pocketing money; after all, it is much riskier for him to pocket money ten times each day as he goes along, than to leave it in the register and collect it all at once at the end of the day.

Liquor Pilferage

A second area of theft is the stealing of liquor and irregularities related to it. Sometimes a bartender will give away free drinks to customers in order to incur their favor and increase their tips. At other times he will give free drinks to fellow workers in exchange for high-cost food items like steaks. Still others, he will remove liquor from the premises either by pouring it into soft drink bottles, by taking the whole bottle and carrying it away with him, or by giving it to an accomplice for removal.

In cases like this, while actual cash is not taken, liquor removal, regardless of what form it takes, obviously decreases restaurant profits, as does steady overpouring. Whether accidental or purposeful, such misdeeds are detrimental to the welfare of a restaurant operation.

In some cases, of course, a bartender may feel that giving a particularly good customer a free drink is good public relations. If this occurs, the bartender should record the drink either on a guest check or on a cash register receipt, giving the reasons for the gratis drink. This way you will be able to control free drinks more closely. At any given time, if there is a major difference between the amount of liquor he has poured and the cash received for it, you should be able to account for it.

What can you do with a bartender who insists he is the host and should be allowed to pour free drinks whenever he feels like it? You should simply advise him that either he complies with your policy or he finds a job with another restaurant that is more lenient. Let everyone know that you mean business on this policy. You might even want to hire observers, known as spotters, to see that it is carried out.

Supposing the bartender gives another form of a freebie by overpouring. Perhaps he'll give a bigger or stronger drink than usual to encourage a customer to leave a larger tip. Or, even more often, he'll feel he can judge the correct amount of liquor for each drink but ends up overpouring instead.

One popular downtown New York bar sold as many as 500 drinks during its peak cocktail hours. The bartender there worked with little supervision and virtually no control devices. Considering himself to be a true professional, the bartender relied on his eyesight to pour the correct amount of liquor into drinks for his customers.

Unfortunately, the bartender tended to pour between 1/8 and 1/16 of an ounce over the exact quantity called for. While this error was unintentional, it resulted in a loss of between two and five quarts of liquor each day during the cocktail hour alone—and cost the bar something in the area of $100 for just that one hour.

To avoid such situations, you should always require the bartender to use a measure. If you want to serve one ounce per drink, use a jigger that gives an ounce to the rim. Or else use a shot glass with a line indicated at just under one ounce. That way your bartenders can pour above the line without giving away too much liquor.

If you provide your bartenders with the proper measuring equipment and standardized recipes, you should either personally supervise it or have someone take the responsibility for seeing that all instructions are followed.

Some bartenders try to conceal theft irregularities by watering down the liquor. This may occur because a waiter has overpoured drinks, failed to ring up drinks sold, or taken some drinks himself.

When one long-time, trusted bartender from a Miami restaurant went on vacation, he was temporarily replaced by a substitute. During the substitute's stint, the management received several complaints from customers that their drinks were watered down.

To make certain that nothing was amiss, the management brought in a spot tester to find out if the bottles were correct according to proof. The tester discovered that several bottles had, as the customers correctly noticed, been watered down, and the bartender was immediately discharged.

Luckily, the tester was not a government or state regulator, so the restaurant was not penalized. Had he been sent by the state to test the liquor instead of being hired by the restaurant, the consequences would have been far worse.

If a restaurant is discovered to have bottles in which the alcohol content per volume of liquor is incorrect, it can lose its liquor license. The state Alcoholic Beverage Commission periodically inspects bottles for proof. If it finds bottles that are under proof, this is grounds for a liquor license suspension that can cripple your business. You may therefore wish to engage a spotter to test alcoholic contents and compliance with the serving and cash-taking procedures as an extra precaution to avoid such goings-on.

Safeguarding the Bar   79

Bringing in Outside Merchandise

Bartenders also cheat restaurants by bringing in their own bottles. In most cases of this kind, the bartenders are trusted employees who have worked in an establishment for some time, know many of the restaurant's clients, and are therefore less suspect than newcomers. To carry out such irregularities, the bartender must also have the opportunity to bring in a bottle from the outside. And he must be able to avoid ringing up the sales for the contents of his particular bottle. A skillful thief will be able to conceal his actions so that there will be no discrepancy between money taken in at the cash register and the liquor inventory.

Regardless of which particular method of pilferage is practiced—and there are others—you, as the owner or operator, should know the detrimental effects of such actions. While stealing is not necessarily limited to the bar alone, it is nevertheless your most vulnerable location and therefore the area of primary control.

Bottle Replacement Control

The most widely used method of protection against pilferage and other irregularities at the bar is the "par stock/bottle replacement/sales value control." This requires that a par stock listing be established at the bar. The par stock listing consists of the number of bottles of each brand required during the business peak period plus one bottle as a margin of safety. The listing of brands and numbers should be posted at the bar. They may also be printed on the bar inventory and requisition form.

Along with this, you should establish a routine whereby the bottles of all bar merchandise should be accumulated throughout the day. Empty bottles should be stored in a box; none should be destroyed. At the end of each business day, the night bartender should record the empties (number of bottles of each brand) on a form like the one on p. 80. This record, prepared in triplicate, should give him the authority to replace the used merchandise on the following day.

WILLIAM ALLEN & CO., N. Y. STOCK FORM 7040

No. 24969

BAR INVENTORY AND REQUISITION

BAR NO._____   DATE_____

LIST NO.	SIZE	DESCRIPTION	PAR STOCK	ON HAND	REQUISITION					INVENTORY	
					QUANT.	UNIT COST	TOTAL COST	UNIT SALE VALUE	TOTAL SALE VALUE	UNIT COST	TOTAL COST

INVENTORY TAKEN BY: _____   ISSUED BY: _____   RECEIVED BY: _____

A person other than the bartender should fill this order and return it with a duplicate copy of the requisition to the bar. The bartender on duty can then check in the merchandise and sign the requisition/issuing record verifying that he has received the bottles recorded.

This record then becomes the basis to calculate the previous day's bar cost and income. This is done by multiplying the number of bottles issued (based on the returned empties of the previous day) times their cost and sales value. The bar cost figures can be derived from the liquor storeroom perpetual inventory control, which will be explained later.

The sales value of each bottle of liquor is calculated by multiplying the number of drinks which can be served from each bottle (based on the ounce size per drink) times its selling price per drink. By multiplying these sales values by the replacement merchandise, after several days required for merchandise turnover, you can estimate the expected bar income and compare it with the actual cash taken in. If there are continuing bar shortages, they should be discussed with the bar personnel to make sure that the sales value calculations are correct and to make them aware of the existing bar control procedures.

Other Security Measures at the Bar

One downtown Chicago hotel relied on its very popular bar for a good part of its income. Over a period of time, the manager noticed a gradual decline in sales. Since the bar was as crowded and busy as ever, he knew that something was wrong.

He began a program of code marking all hotel liquor bottles. Not long after this program began, several uncoded empty bottles of bar gin were turned in for replacements. This happened about three times a week. At that rate, the manager estimated that over a period of a year, the bartender could bring in about 8 cases of liquor from the outside—a loss of between $3,000 and $4,000 a year for the hotel!

A complete package inspection at the employees' entrance helps prevent such deeds as bringing in bottles from the outside. In addition, you should mark your own bottles, either by placing a decal on each of your bottles, or by code marking them with an indelible, invisible marking ink that shows up only under a black light. If you require all old bottles to be turned in for new ones to replace the bar stock, you will very easily be able to spot bottles that come from outside your establishment.

One way to remedy a bartender's failure to ring up a sale is to *insist* that all customers receive a cash register receipt for each drink. For table service, of course, drinks will be written on the guest check. But when customers order drinks at the bar and pay for them there, you should insist that they receive a cash register ticket for every drink purchased. If you check to be sure this is done, it will insure that all drinks will be rung up.

A bartender or anyone else who drinks on the job can cause severe problems. Free drinking can spread and will not only reduce the efficiency of your employees, but will also cause inventory shortages. You should avoid this situation by banning all drinking by employees on the premises. Otherwise, bartenders will be encouraged to slip customers or employees free drinks. Discrepancies will show up eventually, but meanwhile a great deal of damage can be done.

I have been discussing theft practices and controls that occur at the bar itself. But liquor goes through a number of steps—from receiving to storing and issuing—before it ever gets to the bar. Internal thefts may occur at any one of these points, and particular precautions should be taken at each checkpoint.

Receiving

The elements of good receiving include:

1. Counting the number of cases and comparing the count with the quantity shown on the invoices.
2. Making sure that the sizes of bottles delivered are correct.
3. Spot-checking the contents of every fifth case to be sure that all bottles are full and none are broken.

4. Keeping an accurate record of shipments received. This is necessary for your perpetual stock record.

Storing

Before it is issued to the bar, liquor should be stored in a locked storage area. Only one key to this room should be in circulation. If more than one person is authorized to issue liquor from the storeroom to the bar, the same key should be used by both people.

If at all possible, the person in possession of the key should be that person responsible for the liquor; namely, the restaurateur, a trusted employee, or the steward—anyone, that is, *except* the bartender. This is a good way to insure a system of checks and balances.

Issuing and Inventory Control

As previously mentioned, issues to the bar should be made only by the authorization of an assigned requisition, supported by the previous day's empty bottles. If empties cannot be replaced with the same kind of merchandise, you should either adjust the par stock inventory or keep a liquor storeroom record indicating the bottles "owed" the bar. The effectiveness of the issuing system will, however, depend on its strict enforcement.

Based on the issuing records, you should keep a perpetual liquor storeroom inventory on a form like the one on p. 84. One form should be used for each brand and size of all bar merchandise stored. The underlying principle of this inventory control system is that by adding new shipments (number of bottles) and subtracting the bar issues, the "balance"—or stock to be on hand—can be predetermined at any time. This balance should be checked frequently against a physical count of the same brand and bottle size, and should always be checked at the end of each month.

If there are fewer bottles in stock than there should be according to the inventory record, the shortage may be caused

William Allen & Co., N.Y., Stock Form 6198

MAX. _____
MIN. _____

FROM _____ TO _____ 19 ___

STORE ROOM PERPETUAL INVENTORY

COMMODITY: _____
CLASSIFICATION NO. _____
UNIT: _____ LBS.
PRICE PER UNIT: $ _____

Month	Date	on Hand	REC'D	ISSUED	BAL.	Month	Date	on Hand	REC'D	ISSUED	BAL.	Month	Date	on Hand	REC'D	ISSUED	BAL.	REMARKS
	1						1						1					
	2						2						2					
	3						3						3					
	4						4						4					
	5						5						5					
	6						6						6					
	7						7						7					
	8						8						8					
	9						9						9					
	10						10						10					
	11						11						11					
	12						12						12					
	13						13						13					
	14						14						14					
	15						15						15					
	16						16						16					
	17						17						17					
	18						18						18					
	19						19						19					
	20						20						20					
	21						21						21					
	22						22						22					
	23						23						23					
	24						24						24					
	25						25						25					
	26						26						26					
	27						27						27					
	28						28						28					
	29						29						29					
	30						30						30					
	31						31						31					
	Totals						Totals						Totals					
	on Hand						on Hand						on Hand					

by any number of reasons. Among them: pilferage, unrecorded bar or other issues, breakage, or goods invoiced but not received. Obviously, you will want to investigate any of the causes pertaining to your operation and correct them as soon as possible.

Automatic Liquor Dispensing Systems

In addition to the previously described bar control methods, mechanized and electronic bar control systems are finding increasing acceptance among restaurateurs. Whereas the conventional bar control systems alert you to irregularities that have already occurred, they still don't tell you where or how. Automatic dispensing systems, on the other hand, minimize potential irregularities that can occur. Preprogrammed liquor control registers automatically record the price of each drink at the same time that the drink is electronically dispensed. This avoids such irregularities as unrecorded sales, overpouring, or underpouring, and minimizes the possibility of human error.

Some of these devices are designed only to dispense predetermined quantities of liquor. Other more complex systems, which record the price as well, do not release the merchandise until the bartender pushes the proper button at the control register. This assures that every sale is priced accurately and recorded, as well as properly dispensed.

Among the advantages of electronic dispensers are:

• Uniform quantities of liquor dispensed
• Prevention of overpouring and spillage
• Positive inventory control
• Elimination of pricing errors
• Elimination of unrung sales.

As further advances are made in these systems, progressive restaurants owe it to themselves to investigate the possible advantages of this equipment.

7

Additional Operational and Accounting Controls

A once prosperous San Diego restaurant was reduced to the point of near bankruptcy by widespread employee theft. One study estimated that the restaurant was losing as much as 6% of its annual sales to its own employees. A security investigation of the situation revealed virtually no controls or systems to cope with this problem.

For years past the independent restaurant had thrived without controls. "Why should I change now?" asked the owner. "I've always done okay using good old-fashioned methods." The answer was provided by the steadily rising theft losses each year and by the rapidly dwindling profits (which eventually turned into rising deficits).

This is just one example of the complacency that exists in many restaurants when it comes to carefully planned controls. The "good old days" methods simply don't suffice anymore, and today it is in a restaurant's best interests to professionalize with modern control applications.

In a previous chapter I described the leading theft methods. Now let's focus in on preventing such thefts by discouraging employees from trying to use them in the first place. Since an aggressive, frustrated employee will steal if he sees a lack of controls in the restaurant, strict control systems are a must. If an employee knows there is little chance of his being caught, he is far more likely to steal than if he fears discovery. Fear of being caught is a major deterrent to theft.

A manager who does not enforce his company's control policies is practically opening the door to theft. If an employee senses that the restaurant doesn't really care about its cash or merchandise, he may steal without feeling particularly guilty. He can easily determine management's attitude if he sees negligence, carelessness, and indifference in enforcing control systems and in protecting the restaurant's assets.

In some restaurants, management doesn't realize the extent of internal pilferage or the dangers of not keeping it under control. An honest manager may find it hard to believe that his employees will steal. He wants to see only the best qualities in his people. This is usually a healthy attitude. But if a manager consistently rationalizes an employee's actions and insists on believing he is honest even when there are clear indications to the contrary, this can prove quite dangerous.

Because some managers are blind to signs of dishonesty, they may inadvertently set up an atmosphere conducive to theft. They may think that if there are dishonest employees, they will be reported by other employees. Actually, an employee who discovers a coworker stealing tends to take this position: "What Joe does is his own business. I'm hired to do my job here, not to be a detective." He may not feel any guilt or responsibility in the situation. If he dislikes his supervisor or manager, he may even feel happy that someone is "getting even" with the restaurant.

There is also the manager who never really pays much attention to what his employees are doing. He walks through the restaurant thinking or worrying about other things. This kind of manager should have a complete set of control systems and follow up everything he authorizes to make sure he is not being taken advantage of by a dishonest employee. He must be alert to all indications of dishonesty and question anything an employee does that appears unusual. Whenever there is an irregularity, he should undertake a follow-up investigation. If restaurant employees know they will be investigated for any irregularities, they will be working in a disciplined environment. They will see that those who violate company rules will probably be caught.

Usually theft involves a lack of discipline as well as a high level of aggression. If you create a controlled working environment and establish firm policies regarding working conditions, you will be more likely to encourage greater honesty among your employees.

Strong controls prevent theft in a number of different ways. Not only can they reveal the extent of employee thefts, but they can often help discover the culprit. Besides protecting your cash and inventory, they help protect your greatest asset— people.

"In many instances—perhaps the majority—an individual would not have been dishonest had reasonable precautionary methods been exercised," pointed out Virgil W. Peterson, managing director of the Chicago Crime Commission. "To take steps that will successfully prevent this dishonesty is to save many lives from ruin."

The techniques suggested in this chapter will help you plan, organize, and apply these necessary operational controls. They will help you not only to thwart dishonest individuals who exploit weaknesses in your operation, but they will also help you create a more disciplined working environment.

This chapter describes various problem areas in the restaurant where thefts sometimes occur and improvement methods that can help you minimize pilferage. By describing these areas as well as offering possible corrective methods with which to deal with them, this chapter may be able to help you initiate and improve your controls in these areas.

Package Controls

The innocent-looking waitress would always carry packages in and out of the restaurant when she started and finished her shifts at a Dallas restaurant. Surprising as it may seem, nobody thought anything of it—probably because of the regularity with which it occurred. One night, however, a supervisor insisted on checking one of her packages as she was leaving the restaurant. He discovered a few salt shakers. A follow-up investigation revealed that everything from steaks to spoons had been going out the door with her for months.

How can you curtail the smuggling of stolen items out of your restaurant in packages? One school of thought maintains that no packages should be allowed in or out of the restaurant under any conditions. This may seem to be an extreme solution, but it may be necessary and often saves a lot of aggravation. If you do allow packages, you should not permit them to come in and out of your restaurant indiscriminately. Here are some package controls you might want to use that should not offend honest employees, but often deter the guilty ones:

1. A supervisor should conduct a package inspection at the door where the employees leave. Perhaps this could be a spot check where a few packages are selected for inspection each night. One night it might be one-quarter of the packages; another night, one-tenth. The point is to let all employees know they might be caught at any time if they are stealing. But no one is delayed too long nor subject to constant search every night. (Lengthy delays might create more employee hostility than a search would be worth.)

2. You should require all employees to leave their packages open and unsealed. This enables the supervisor either to see the contents or to check them if he so desires and acts as a psychological deterrent. A potential thief would know that his open package could be examined at any time. If you know generally what is inside a package and have regular inspections, you can prevent most package thefts. Then when you see employees leaving work, you'll know they're not leaving with some of your valuable inventory.

3. You might also require employees to leave all incoming packages at the entrance, in an office, or in a central room, and to pick them up only when they leave. This would greatly reduce the opportunity for them to slip anything into these packages.

Only One Exit

For maximum control, you should designate one door—and one door only—as the authorized employee entrance and exit. This should be used by all part-time as well as full-time employees. It might be the same door that customers use, but it should never be a door at a receiving area. Having one controlled, designated entrance and exit will prevent employees from slipping items into their cars by leaving through an unwatched exit. (Since people sometimes hide stolen merchandise in their cars, asking for their license plate numbers on your personnel form may also be a deterrent to theft.)

One of the favorite escape routes of dishonest employees is through an unauthorized door. You should check all unauthorized exits periodically to see if employees may be using them to take out stolen items. This is most likely to happen during a work break or just before closing time. You should consider putting reliable people near these doors to keep tabs on what is happening.

Employees are usually required to leave a restaurant through a specific exit where they can be observed. But this kind of system can be exploited. An employee walking out of the same exit nonchalantly every evening can be carrying all types of items with him, but may go unchallenged because the supervisor at that exit is so accustomed to seeing the same employee every evening at the same.

Employees will sometimes walk through unauthorized exits with stolen merchandise. If a supervisor spots this, he may be afraid to challenge the employee, either because of fear or because he doesn't want to antagonize the employee. Here again, a regular package inspection at an authorized exit will allow a supervisor to check for stolen items more easily and with a minimum amount of anxiety.

You should also make a careful inspection of your premises to see which windows are the most likely for employees to toss out items for later pickup. Where or on which roof are such items likely to land? You might conduct spot checks on the window and roof areas or have a few trusted employees keep a careful watch on these spots. You might also want to keep a number of windows locked or screened permanently and rely on air conditioning and other ventilation for fresh air.

Exchanging Stolen Items

In a Houston restaurant, two waitresses on the same shift worked out a theft routine using the locker room as their base. Each had a duplicate key to the other's locker. Each would leave whichever items she managed to swipe in the other's locker. Later, each would carry the items from her own locker out of the restaurant in her handbag when she finished her shift.

The idea of being part of the gang, or of gaining the approval of fellow workers by stealing and then exchanging it with fellow employees seems to have a certain appeal and excitement. Sometimes the situation can become so flagrant that employees will even exchange stolen items at will, depending on their preferences.

Locker Room Security

A locker room is necessary for employees to change their clothes and store their personal belongings. But it also is a theft hazard where employees can hide items in coats, handbags, and the like, or where they can exchange stolen items with each other. Steps should be taken to make the locker room more secure and to show employees that you mean business in your theft prevention programs.

Sometimes the locker room where employees change their clothes is used as a storage area for stolen merchandise. An employee can accumulate items in the restaurant, go into the locker room when he finishes his shift, and either stuff the items under his clothes or wrap them in a package. He can then take these items out of the restaurant and get away with them if nobody challenges him.

Try to keep the lighting in the locker room as bright as possible; nothing encourages thievery more than a dimly lit room. You should periodically check to see that the lights are bright enough, and you should put a clip on the panel for the locker room lights so that nobody can switch them off without a key.

Another important precaution is discouraging your employees from leaving valuables in their lockers. You should emphasize to all employees the importance of keeping their own lockers locked at all times. Under no conditions should employees be allowed to carry coats or handbags from the locker room into the storage area or any other place where there is food or money. Coats should be kept in the locker room or some other designated central place.

Control of Keys

Management should carefully guard against theft or duplication of any and all keys. One restaurant manager left his keys on a stockroom shelf. An employee spotted them, ran out and had several duplicates cut while on his coffee break, and returned the keys to the same spot so that the manager never missed them. Then he sold the duplicate keys to a local gang of hoodlums. One moonlight night at about 3 A.M. not too long afterwards, the gang rented a truck, backed it up to the restaurant's rear door, and helped themselves to every food and supply item they could find. The result: $24,000 in losses for the restaurant.

In Portland, Ore., a porter slipped into the maintenance department one lunch hour, opened the maintenance supervisor's locker, and took a key off the ring. He duplicated it at a nearby store and then replaced it on the supervisor's key ring. Almost every night for months afterwards, the porter would return to the restaurant after it had closed, unlock the side door, and fill his trunk with foodstuffs. Finally, a passing police patrol became suspicious of his actions and reported him to management. He was arrested shortly afterwards—but only after he had cost the restaurant some $20,000 in stolen food items.

If particular care is not given to watching keys, your restaurant can experience all kinds of unanticipated problems.

One California restaurant kept careful records and had an effective perpetual inventory system. So shortages of a particularly expensive scotch that amounted to five or six bottles each month were discovered very quickly and traced to the storage area.

At first the management suspected the head bartender, who was the only person besides the owner who had a key to the storeroom. But upon questioning, the bartender remembered that the owner's son had borrowed the key. As it turned out, the owner's son had duplicated it and helped himself to a bottle whenever he wanted. While he felt justified in doing so, his actions resulted in unfair suspicions and unbalanced records.

Careless handling of keys can make it easy for anyone to enter the premises illegally. Keys should be given only to employees who must have them to perform specific functions. These employees should turn in their keys at a special control key box next to the employee exit when they leave each night. This will help a restaurant account for all its keys.

Should the early morning cook need the key to open up, it may be necessary to make an exception to this rule. However, only under absolutely unavoidable circumstances should you allow a key to be taken from the premises.

It is wise to keep a record of the few keys that you do issue. And you should exercise the same care with each key as you would with a $100 bill. Here are some precautions you can take:

1. Avoid situations that could lead to key duplication. Caution supervisors not to leave restaurant keys with parking lot attendants, lying around the office or storeroom, or inside coats and coat jackets that are hanging in the office.
2. Keep complete records on key distribution so you know how many keys have been issued and to whom.
3. If a key is lost or an employee leaves without turning in his key, you may have to put a new lock on that door.
4. Don't allow anyone other than a member of your top management team access to the master key.

5. Make sure that every lock has a different key, so that one key will not open every lock.

6. Never use a key chain with a tag carrying the restaurant's name and address. This can be an open invitation to anyone who finds it. Instead, code each key and inform only authorized personnel what the code means.

7. Conduct periodic inventories of all keys. Have supervisors and other employees show you each key so you know it hasn't been misplaced, lost, or stolen.

8. Change locks to storage areas periodically as a preventive measure.

Remember that a thief with a key to your restaurant or stockrooms can designate himself as a business partner very quickly and help put you out of business. Furthermore, your insurance policy may not cover thefts occurring through negligence such as the loss of a key. So a strong key control system should be a major part of your security planning.

Trash Removal

Since a trash can is one of the favorite places for sneaking items out of a restaurant for later pickup, your control procedures must take this into account. You should make sure a supervisor or security person is present when trash is loaded onto a truck. Whenever possible, it's a good idea to spot check outgoing trash carefully for items that may be hidden in it.

Even if you burn trash in your own incinerator, the incinerator room and the people who run it ought to be checked periodically. You might test the man in the incinerator room by tossing a perfectly good silverware piece in with the trash to see if he reports finding it. If he doesn't, you should caution him to be more careful in the future.

Burglar Alarm Systems

As added protection, many restaurants use burglar alarm systems to prevent intruders from entering and vandalizing the premises and taking valuable merchandise. These systems are designed so that an intruder who enters the restaurant after closing hours will set off an alarm bell. Often the bell is enough to scare off would-be burglars. However, at the same time, a signal is sent to the alarm company's central office, which then sends out men to investigate the cause of the signal. Burglar alarm systems are an important and basic way of deterring intruders.

Closed-Circuit TV?

My feeling is that generally there is more to be lost than gained in installing closed-circuit TV to catch thieves. The amount of antagonism aroused by such a system might incite some employees to challenge it rather than to be frightened by it.

Nevertheless, there are situations where closed-circuit TV can be of immense help, particularly if you suspect one or more employees of stealing. But it must be used properly in a specific situation so as not to cause a hostile reaction among the employees.

If you do use closed-circuit TV, you could temporarily conceal it in a fixture and watch the suspected employee on a monitor. This is more effective than observing the person at close range, where he will know you are watching him.

Integrity Shoppers

A number of restaurants employ "comparison shoppers" on a full-time or part-time basis. These shoppers, who are not known to restaurant personnel, eat in the units periodically and file full reports on such matters as the quality of the food, the caliber, speed, and courtesy of service, and the overall atmosphere and cleanliness of the restaurant. They usually also give performance ratings to waitresses and cashiers.

In view of the severe internal theft problems that some restaurant companies are encountering, it might be wise to give such shoppers an additional task of testing the honesty of the waitress and cashier as well. Some restaurants may already be doing this without publicizing it, but using experienced, anonymous shoppers to test your up-front control systems would seem to be a practical measure. After all, protecting your restaurants from pilferage can be even more important to your profits than serving high quality food to your customers with a smile and in a perfect restaurant environment.

Internal Accounting Controls

A good internal controls system has cross-checks for every major control procedure. As a rule, the person who does the ordering should not be the same as the person who approves invoice payments. The degree of separation of responsibilities depends on the size of the food service. In a small operation, the manager or owner may become a part-time internal auditor, checking transactions, confirming items, and investigating original documents. However, regardless of size, here are the basic ingredients of a good internal control program in such situations:

1. Deposit all cash receipts intact daily.
2. Make all payments by bank check and countersign them.
3. Personally reconcile bank account statements each month.
4. Spot check your bank balances during different periods of each month.
5. Check outgoing customer statements yourself occasionally against accounts receivable, and then mail them.

6. Receive and open all incoming mail yourself occasionally.

7. Compare all cash receipts with your own books and with the deposits shown on the bank statement.

8. Dont't let the bookkeeper do receiving and shipping of items.

9. Approve general entries yourself, especially if they relate to sales allowances or bad debts.

10. Bond the bookkeeper for a suitable amount of money.

11. Be sure your mail is opened by a trusted employee other than the cashier or cash receivables bookkeeper.

12. Have the person who opens the mail prepare a list of all mail received. It should be classified as to bank checks, money orders, stamps, etc. Compare this list frequently with the cash receipt book ledger.

13. Keep controls on all sales and possible rebates.

14. Record interest payments, rents, and other miscellaneous income so that any failure to get a receipt can be investigated if necessary.

15. Handle credit card disbursement requests promptly.

16. Try to have the duties of a cashier, accounts receivable bookkeeper, and general bookkeeper performed by different people as a cross-check against each other.

17. Make sure that your cash is physically safeguarded.

18. Have the general bookkeeper maintain a detailed record of negotiable notes and securities, and have a third party hold the actual documents so that comparisons can be made.

19. Be extremely careful about petty cash disbursements and require attached documentation.

20. Be careful about check distribution. It might help you to ask yourself a number of questions: Are all your bank checks on safety paper, serially prenumbered, and accounted for? Are all your checks written in permanent ink or by a check-writing machine? Are you certain at the time of signing that your checks are

completed except for the signature, and that they are accompanied by supporting documents on which the check number and payment date appear in ink? Do you always prohibit the drawing of checks for cash and the signing of checks in advance?

21. Pay all payrolls strictly by bank check. This helps you to keep a complete record of them.

22. Occasionally audit your pay rates to make sure the proper amounts are actually being paid to each employee.

23. Distribute pay envelopes to employees yourself occasionally.

24. See that all purchases are authorized by a responsible person and that all purchase invoices are approved for payment only upon evidence of receipt of the items. Receipt of all inventories should be in written form and numerically controlled. Purchasing, receiving, and storeroom functions should, if at all possible, be performed by different people who can be held responsible for discrepancies in their individual areas.

25. Be sure that purchase and sales invoices are checked over for the following: quantity received, prices, terms, shipping charges, additions and extensions, and dates on purchase invoices.

26. Be sure to have credit memos made out for all returned merchandise and signed by a deliveryman.

27. Besides perpetual inventories on high-cost items, make periodic, unannounced inventory counts of other items.

28. Be sure to place responsibility for inventory shortages or overages on the appropriate employees. See that adjustments for inventory differences are approved by responsible people.

29. Have people other than those who keep the cash records reconcile monthly bank statements and cancelled checks with the general books.

30. Examine cancelled checks, signatures, and endorse-

ments, and return the checks to the bank where necessary. Note deposit dates on the bank statements and compare them with deposit dates shown on your cash receipt records.

31. Be sure that all credits to accounts other than those arising from cash remittances and cash discounts receive approval from an authority other than the cashier or accounts receivable bookkeeper.

32. Make sure a responsible executive authorizes any writing off of bad debts.

33. Keep complete control over records of bad debts that are less than three years old.

34. Mail customers a special statement at least once a year to be sure they agree with the accounts receivable records. Such a mailing should be initiated by your auditor.

35. Require all employees to take vacations which they are entitled to. Be sure their duties are covered by other employees.

36. Be sure that accounting methods, routines, and control systems are detailed in written instructions.

37. Change the combination on your safe periodically.

Outside Audits

Outside audits would seem to provide the maximum in controls for a restaurant, but there is a question as to their practical effects. One Michigan chain for years depended on outside audits to uncover inventory and cash shortages and correct problems. But in the face of continually rising shortages, this chain was forced to admit that the outside audits could have been handled a lot more effectively.

Auditors sometimes feel that their prime loyalty is to the auditing group rather than to the whole company. They tend correctly to consider themselves outside the organization. This may be a natural result of their usually being rewarded for finding things wrong rather than for helping people do better work.

An auditor's objectives are sometimes the opposite of a restaurant manager's. An auditor tends to be a perfectionist. He focuses on specific problems in-depth, while a manager tends to look for workable rather than perfect solutions. The manager focuses on getting the entire job done rather than perfecting one part of it. For example, the auditor may be tempted to evaluate the operation and propose solutions, while the manager prefers to get feedback and to work out his own solutions.

As a result of these factors, the following situations may occur when outside auditors are in the picture:

1. The manager tends to pay attention to doing well in those areas that will be measured by an auditor, whether or not they are important to his goals.

2. The manager puts great effort into trying to conceal problems and imperfections.

3. Top management tends to use auditing information about subordinates in an unintentionally punitive way. It conducts constant inquiries which give subordinates the feeling of having bosses on their back all the time, even when the subordinates themselves are trying to correct the problems. Audits can become a frustrating, threatening element in the working environment.

4. The manager and those below him may try to falsify and distort information to avoid criticism and punishment.

5. Detailed information gathered by auditors tends to be passed too far up the line in both the auditing function and the management organization. The information is then available only to people who are too far removed from the problem to properly evaluate it.

To correct these deficiencies, auditing can be improved to gain real benefits. Here are some suggestions:

1. Have as much line involvement as possible. Let your supervisors help decide which areas of performance are

to be audited and how the information gathered is to be used.

2. Use horizontal rather than vertical reporting. The more the information gathered is made available directly to the man with the problem, the more likely that it will be effective. The information should be made available to higher levels only if the problem is not corrected. Under this system, people on your staff will not only be less motivated to hide or falsify information, but also less likely to feel threatened.

3. Reward auditors or consultants for helping rather than for finding fault.

4. Initiate useful feedback. The faster the auditing information is fed back, the more useful it will be to the line organization.

In short, the use of outside auditors and consultants can be beneficial if handled in a positive, constructive manner that will help rather than hinder a restaurant operation.

Closing Precautions

Perhaps the most critical period in your theft controls occurs when you close for the night. You should be sure that all storage rooms are locked, that nobody is hiding in the rest rooms or lockers, that the night lights are on, food and beverages have been stored and secured, windows and doors are locked, and that any alarm system has been activated.

You might conduct a quick inspection of the entire building just in case an employee is hiding in a rest room, closet, or some other inconspicuous place. Internal pilferage can be extremely dangerous, because you're very unlikely to catch a thief who is in the building when nobody is there.

An alarm system is one defense against a "hide-in" thief. Otherwise, he can operate in relative safety for hours. Since most valuables are in the back of the house—an area usually hidden from the street—a thief who has escaped discovery at closing time can literally wipe you out in one night. Even if you do have an alarm system, it's a good idea to triple-check the premises at closing time.

Summary of Additional Operational and Accounting Controls

Here then are the main general controls systems that you can use to prevent internal pilferage in some of the problem areas of your restaurant:

1. Spot-check all incoming and outgoing employee packages.
2. Designate and enforce only one employee entrance and exit.
3. Conduct periodic spot checks to be sure all windows and doors are in good working order.
4. Keep a careful eye on the locker room.
5. Make sure all keys are accounted for.
6. Check the trash occasionally.
7. Install burglar alarm system if at all possible.
8. Use closed-circuit TV under particular circumstances if warranted.
9. Consider the use of integrity shoppers and outside audits.
10. Walk through every area of the restaurant yourself whenever possible.
11. Exercise vigilance in the receiving and storage areas of your restaurant.
12. Conduct monthly inventories, and keep a steady running inventory of as many items as you can.
13. Be your own best auditor, and establish and enforce complete internal controls.

Even with the best control systems in the world, however, employee theft is still possible. Although sharp controls will often discourage potential theives and expose thefts in the early stages, a determined thief is hard to stop. There is no absolute deterrent against a human being who craves something for nothing. Thus we need maximum internal controls and supervision if we hope to make real inroads in internal theft.

8

Cash Register Controls

Two boys came up to the cash register to pay for their lunches. Since both boys had ordered a hamburger and a coke, their checks were identical. The cashier rang the first amount on the cash register and handed the first boy his change. When the second boy paid his check, the cashier also handed him his change. No one even noticed that the second check was never rung up on the register or that the second check was thrown in the waste basket. After all, the correct amount was shown on the register already. Later that day when the restaurant was quiet, the cashier pocketed the amount of the lunch and cleared the cash register that night.

This practice—called *bunching checks*—is one of the most common in fast food operations. When two or more identical checks are presented, the cashier can do one of two things, depending on the amount of cash he receives. If he gets the exact amount of the check, he can simply pocket the money. If he gets more, he can put it in the register, give the customer change, and pocket the amount of the meal. Since this check isn't punched, the cash register will balance at the end of the day. This may cost the restaurant many hundreds of dollars each year.

One of the reasons this practice is so dangerous is that it can go undetected for years. It is one of the commonest ways of "beating the system." Beating the system is one of the more sophisticated ways of stealing from the cash register.

Of course, there are those cashiers who simply dip into the cash register and take a certain amount of money. But this is usually detected very quickly, since the day's total checks don't jibe with the amount in the cash register. If this happens more than one or two days in a row, a manager will figure out that theft is causing the problem rather quickly. When cashiers figure out ways to beat the system, however, the day's checks match the cash in the register, so it may be months or even years before their thefts are caught.

In another restaurant in Tampa, Fla., one cashier consistently allowed his friends free meals. Sometimes he simply overlooked them when they walked out the door with their checks without paying. Other times they carried their checks to the register, asked for change of a dollar, waited for the register to ring open and shut and for an exchange of money at the cash register, and walked out, either taking their checks with them or leaving the cashier to dispose of it.

One way of stopping the practice of bunching checks or of giving free meals to friends is to have all checks numbered consecutively. That way, if any checks are missing or lost, they will be noticed immediately and looked into. A cashier will be unable to throw out a check and pocket the money if every check must be accounted for.

Numbered checks or blocks of checks should be issued to service personnel, who sign for them on a waiter signature sheet. At the end of the day, each waiter's guest checks can be checked off against a consecutive number record like the one on p. 107. In this way, you can detect any missing checks and trace them to the specific service personnel.

If you don't have numbered checks, it's particularly important to take extra precautions. One principle you should always follow is to physically locate the cash register in a position that is highly visible both to customers and to the managers. That way the cashier will have a great deal more difficulty in throwing out checks or in ringing identical checks only once. Also be sure to locate the cashier near the door so that custom-

CONSECUTIVE NUMBER RECORD

HUNDRED_____   SERIES_____

WM. ALLEN & CO., STOCK FORM 7029

00	50	00	50	00	50	00	50	00	50
	51	1	51	1	51	1	51	1	51
2	52	2	52	2	52	2	52	2	52
3	53	3	53	3	53	3	53	3	53
4	54	4	54	4	54	4	54	4	54
5	55	5	55	5	55	5	55	5	55
6	56	6	56	6	56	6	56	6	56
7	57	7	57	7	57	7	57	7	57
8	58	8	58	8	58	8	58	8	58
9	59	9	59	9	59	9	59	9	59
10	60	10	60	10	60	10	60	10	60
11	61	11	61	11	61	11	61	11	61
12	62	12	62	12	62	12	62	12	62
13	63	13	63	13	63	13	63	13	63
14	64	14	64	14	64	14	64	14	64
15	65	15	65	15	65	15	65	15	65
16	66	16	66	16	66	16	66	16	66
17	67	17	67	17	67	17	67	17	67
18	68	18	68	18	68	18	68	18	68
19	69	19	69	19	69	19	69	19	69
20	70	20	70	20	70	20	70	20	70
21	71	21	71	21	71	21	71	21	71
22	72	22	72	22	72	22	72	22	72
23	73	23	73	23	73	23	73	23	73
24	74	24	74	24	74	24	74	24	74
25	75	25	75	25	75	25	75	25	75
26	76	26	76	26	76	26	76	26	76
27	77	27	77	27	77	27	77	27	77
28	78	28	78	28	78	28	78	28	78
29	79	29	79	29	79	29	79	29	79
30	80	30	80	30	80	30	80	30	80
31	81	31	81	31	81	31	81	31	81
32	82	32	82	32	82	32	82	32	82
33	83	33	83	33	83	33	83	33	83
34	84	34	84	34	84	34	84	34	84
35	85	35	85	35	85	35	85	35	85
36	86	36	86	36	86	36	86	36	86
37	87	37	87	37	87	37	87	37	87
38	88	38	88	38	88	38	88	38	88
39	89	39	89	39	89	39	89	39	89
40	90	40	90	40	90	40	90	40	90
41	91	41	91	41	91	41	91	41	91
42	92	42	92	42	92	42	92	42	92
43	93	43	93	43	93	43	93	43	93
44	94	44	94	44	94	44	94	44	94
45	95	45	95	45	95	45	95	45	95
46	96	46	96	46	96	46	96	46	96
47	97	47	97	47	97	47	97	47	97
48	98	48	98	48	98	48	98	48	98
49	99	49	99	49	99	49	99	49	99

ers have to walk directly by the register as they leave. This enables a supervisor stationed there to ask any customer to pay his bill on the way out if the cashier doesn't do so.

Even numbered checks don't eliminate "beating the system," however. In one busy New York restaurant, each waiter received a numbered check and was responsible for that check and the total amount due from a corresponding dinner table. One careless waiter dropped his checks, which were picked up by another waiter. The second waiter presented the check to the table that was not his, collected and pocketed the money, said good evening to the customers, and dropped the check on the floor. When the careless waiter discovered his table customers gone and his check on the floor, it was too late for him to do anything about the situation. He was held responsible for this carelessness and fired shortly afterwards.

In such cases, restaurant policies vary as far as holding waiters responsible and accountable for customer payment. However, accountability goes a long way in decreasing theft and increasing the employee's alertness and sense of responsibility.

Since restaurants depend so heavily on cash transactions, the problem is particularly acute. Money, rather than checks or credit cards, usually passes back and forth, and there is plenty of room for either error or deliberate theft. Honest as well as dishonest mistakes can be made in adding the check or in making change. Either way, the restaurant may lose.

Establish Accountability

Accountability is the essential ingredient of cash register controls. To employees this means being responsible, answerable, and accountable. To management, it means being able to locate the source of a problem when checking back on any transaction. Effective accountability must establish a complete unbroken line from the customer to the restaurant's bank deposit. Thus control systems are needed to establish lines between the accounting department and the cashier or his supervisor. Each person in the line should know that he can be held responsible for anything that occurs at a particular time.

Accountability becomes even more important in the newer, more complex multiple line cash registers and computerized terminal systems of modern fast food operations. Anywhere from three to twelve cashiers can be on duty at any given time under this system. All too often, a fast food operation doesn't keep track of which cashier is on which register at specific times throughout the day. Admittedly this presents problems; personnel has to shift positions in the operation rapidly and sometimes unpredictably to handle the changing flow of traffic.

But whether the registers are computerized or manual, it is essential to develop a system of strict accountability for each register. Otherwise, you'll face the same situation as one fast food chain, which doubled its volume through the speedier, faster-turn, multiple line terminals, but suffered a profit dip because of unaccounted losses at the terminals. "How could we know which cashier was at a particular terminal when the money disappeared, and how could we even know which terminal the losses came from?" one operations manager asked.

To establish accountability, you should give each cashier a separate cash drawer. If you allow more than one cashier to work from the same cash drawer, you can't prove who took any missing cash. You can be assured of identification through a special code on the tape for each cashier who uses the register. Or if possible, you can simply have the cashier sign his name and time on the detail tape when he starts or finishes on the register.

Some restaurants require a cashier to count and sign for the cash he receives at the start of his shift. When he finishes, he again counts the cash and turns in a tally sheet showing his total. In other restaurants, he merely deposits the cash in the drawer, which is then counted by a second person. In any case, it's a good idea not to give him access to the total sales figure when the supervisor or manager takes the reading. Nor should he be given any clue as to how much money he should have taken in during his shift. A tip like this might give him a chance to take some money and then adjust his figures before he can be caught.

As an added precaution each cashier should have his own key to the register and his own identifying number on each check. These checks should be compared with the cash receipts on the machine tape and with the final cash count. After the cashier ends his shift, the supervisor should remove the cash drawer and make sure all the cash is counted. Although this activity is time consuming, it is well worth the effort.

Management should always be sure that a cashier starts off each day with a different bank of cash. A cashier should never be allowed to keep the same bank of money from the previous day. Instead, management should get the money out of the restaurant and into a bank at the end of every day and as frequently during the day as feasible. If you do have to keep money on hand between deposits, try to keep it in a locked safe that has an alarm system. A large sum of money kept in a restaurant is an open invitation for internal as well as external theft.

Mistakes and frustrations leading to thievery can also result from employee fatigue. Try not to keep the same cashier on the job hour after hour. He should be given a reasonable amount of time for a break. This helps keep him well-fit for the demands of the job and prevents hostility from building up against management.

Most emphatically, accountability requires the manager or supervisor to clearly notify each cashier of any violation of restaurant policy or of any shortages or overages in his previous day's work. The manager should regularly review overages and shortages with each cashier. That way any discrepancies don't get too far out of hand, and the cashiers know that errors will be detected immediately and that it will be difficult to get away with anything.

Clear Rules

You should establish definite control rules that are easily understood before assigning anyone to a cash register. When you hire a cashier, give him a written copy of the rules and have him sign a carbon copy. This will confirm that the rules have been reviewed with him, that he understands them, and that he agrees to abide by them.

One dishonest cashier may quickly drain away some of your profits if there are no rules or the rules aren't enforced. How strictly should the rules be in the first place? It's up to you to find a balance between the effects of control on customer service, productivity, employee morale, and the amount of loss that can be recovered through various types of controls. Here are some rules that you can adapt to your own cash handling situation and your own individual operating philosophy:

1. Every sale must be rung in the right sequence and the right amount. This is the only way to be sure of keeping track of each transaction and of eliminating potential alibis.

2. In cases where the cashier himself is adding a series of items, such as in a fast food operation, he might call out the price of each item as he records it on the register. This reassures the customer that there is no overcharge and makes bunching checks difficult.

3. No pens or pencils should be allowed at the cash register. They make it too easy for cashiers to alter records on the spot.

4. The release lever inside the register must not be used to open the cash drawer. If a customer asks for change, a "no sale" or "no change" key should be rung to open the drawer. The right-hand door or back panel which houses the release trigger for opening the drawer should be kept locked at all times. Only the manager should have the key.

5. Detail tapes should be replaced immediately if they run out. When there is no detail tape, there is a period of time in which the restaurant has no printed record of the transactions to uncover theft manipulations. Detail tapes should be checked at the start of each day and replaced if the supply gets low.

6. Cash registers should be kept locked when not in use. Any unlocked, unattended register is an open invitation to steal. Never leave the register unattended.

7. If a cashier needs change, only a supervisor should bring it to him. If the cashier goes to the office to get change, he could stop in the lavatory, pocket any stolen money, and dispose of checks.

8. Any void or overring should be approved by the manager or supervisor. One of the favorite cashier theft methods is to write fake overring error slips, put them in the register, and remove an equal amount of cash.

Most food service operations do not normally give cash receipts to customers. This makes theft even more tempting for a cashier, since customers won't know the difference. This is one of the reasons why a careful auditing procedure is such an important security measure.

Auditing Techniques

Late one night the new manager of a large Des Moines restaurant scanned the register detail tapes of the day's transactions. He noticed that one of the tapes periodically indicated a "no sale" ring and that rerings of errors indicated on error slips were not on other tapes. After a thorough review of previous detail tapes, the manager found conclusive proof that three of his cashiers were stealing money. Within a week of the apprehension of these cashiers, the restaurant's cash shortages dipped drastically.

Itemized detail tapes can be one of the most effective theft control devices available, since they can help find clues to dishonesty. Auditing cash register operations means completely examining and reviewing all records of the transactions. Rather than assuming that a transaction is legitimate, you should check it completely.

Here are key points to watch for when you examine register detail tapes:

1. *Continuity of transaction numbers.* A break in the continuity of transaction numbers can be a clue that a dishonest employee is at work. Perhaps he closes out he register early in the evening, then reopens it with a fresh tape and a fresh bank of cash. He rings up all transactions for the next few hours but pockets the money and destroys the detail tape. This can happen when a manager doesn't check each day's tapes to see that there is a continuity in transaction numbers between the previous day's tape and the new one.

2. *Overages or shortages.* A series of small overages could actually be more dangerous than an occasional shortage.

Errors could cause shortages and may simply indicate that the person isn't properly trained or doesn't have the necessary accuracy. But overages, paradoxically, are more likely to indicate manipulation and possible dishonesty. A pattern of daily small overages with an occasional large overage could indicate that the cashier has been underringing and can't remove the money, so it remains in the register as a substantial overage.

Or, if a cashier underrings and steals the accumulated money from the underrings, he may carefully avoid taking the full amount of his unrecorded sales for fear that it will leave a shortage in his register, which could draw management's attention. Thus he leaves a small amount of extra money in the register, feeling that an overage is safer than a shortage.

3. *Blank spots.* Blank spots where no figures appear when they should may be caused by a skipping of the cash register mechanism. But they may indicate that the register was opened without the record of that opening being printed onto the detail tape.

A restaurant manager who can analyze his cash register detail tapes carefully may find a dishonest cashier's tape to be as much of a confession as if he had written the confession and signed his name to it.

Surprise Audits

A surprise cash register audit can sometimes uncover theft immediately and make employees aware that surprise audits could be conducted at any time. If you suspect a certain cashier, have the supervisor move in suddenly during a lull period, close the register for a minute, remove the cash tray and register detail tape, and replace the detail tape and tray with a new bank. The cashier can resume handling customers immediately. Or, if you have two cash registers, you can shut down one to check the detail tape and cash drawer.

A supervisor should take the detail tape and cash drawer to the office for balancing. If major overages or shortages appear, an immediate investigation should be launched into the situation to determine whether the cashier is merely making errors or whether he is stealing from the restaurant.

Supervision Required

The manager, assistant manager, or supervisor should be designated to keep an eye on the cash register at all times. Perhaps this responsibility can be divided among two or three persons, but the signals should be clear as to who is watching at any given time. A cashier who knows he is being watched will find it hard to try stealing even if he wants to, and the majority of cashiers who are honest will not mind the extra attention. Keeping a close watch over the cash register entails very little extra effort and adds an element of efficiency to the operation that helps prevent mistakes and losses.

If you select a cashier supervisor, the person should be completely trained and able to direct people. He should be the one who makes sure that the cashier rules are followed. He should watch for any unrecorded sales and for open cash drawers. He should be able to insure that any cash register not being used is locked, that handbags and packages are kept away from the register, and that all overrings, voids, no sales, and credits are approved. In a multiple line system of several cash registers, the supervisor's job of keeping an eye on all the registers becomes even more crucial.

It's also a good idea for the cashier supervisor to try to meet friends and relatives of employees at company social functions. He should then acknowledge or speak to these friends or relatives whenever they come into the restaurant. This lets the cashier know he recognizes them and may possibly be looking extra carefully when they come to the register to pay their bill.

If the supervisor sees a cashier violate a restaurant policy rule he should call the employee into the office and advise him that such conduct won't be tolerated. He could write up the violation, but the main thing is to call it to the employee's attention. The cashier supervisor is responsible for letting his employees know that he is aware of what is happening and that he cares about the restaurant and its people. The worst thing he can do is ignore a violation of rules and hope that it won't happen again.

It's especially important for the supervisor to give each cashier personal attention. This is the best way to combat the apathy, disinterest, or frustration that emerge from a lack of attention. These kinds of feelings lead to such thinking as: "With all this money around, who's going to miss a few dollars? Management doesn't care about me or the money anyway." By making his employees feel that he cares about both them and his restaurant, a supervisor can inspire a feeling of responsibility and care among personnel.

Summary of Precautions

Here then are the prime requirements to curb theft at your cash registers:

1. Have a system of numbered checks wherever possible, and at least periodically search for missing checks by accounting for them in consecutively numbered seence.
2. Locate the cash register in a strategic position near the exit.
3. Establish complete accountability for each cashier at each register.
4. Establish a clear set of control rules for cashiers, and stick to these rules.
5. Use the detail tapes to look for clues of possible dishonesty.
6. Conduct surprise audits on a cash register periodically.
7. Assign a specific person to supervise the cash register operation and to watch it carefully.

Perhaps the ideal solution is to have only one cash register and one control point. This might be an easy solution except in some of the higher volume food service operations that need more than one register. In any case, remember that a cash register that constantly jingles with money is a tempting theft target for your employees. While most cashiers are honest, you can't take chances when this much money is at stake. Generally a cashier steals largely because it seems so easy. Your job is to convince him that management is aware of what is happening and cares!

PART 4

Investigative Techniques

9

Undercover Detectives

Walter Jones, manager of an Atlanta restaurant, was at his wit's end. His repeated efforts to halt stockroom thefts were still meeting with discouraging results. He had been working on the problem ever since his assistant brought it to his attention six months earlier. He had tried everything he could think of, but each week inventory losses continued to mount.

Finally, in desperation and consternation, Walter decided to start again. He hired a carpenter to build a special new stockroom that looked like a fortress and was fortified with a heavy oak door. He bought an expensive, heavy steel padlock that was guaranteed to thwart the most professional lock pick. As an absolute precaution, he had the two keys that came with the lock stamped "Do Not Duplicate." He entrusted one key to his assistant and kept the other on his own key ring clipped to his belt.

He also set up extensive control procedures for the new stockroom. Only his assistant and one other trusted supervisor could remove any items from the stockroom. A running inventory record pad was tacked inside the stockroom door, and whenever items were removed from the locked area, the exact number of items, and the type and identifying brand were noted on the pad.

Walter waited eight weeks and then one day walked confidently to the stockroom to check his inventory. He had gone over the entire plan in his mind many times in the last two months. There were no possible loopholes. The stock simply had to balance. But would it?

Upon reaching the stockroom door, he carefully examined the lock. He found no scratches or any other signs of a picked or forced entry. He carefully checked the hasp and the edges of the door. Still no telltale marks. By now Walter was beaming. It certainly seemed as if he had defeated the thieves. Next he carefully checked the actual stock against the inventory sheets tacked on the wall. He took a full hour and even opened some of the cartons to confirm that what was marked on them was actually in them. With a feeling of accomplishment, he finally took the inventory withdrawal pad, snapped the heavy padlock shut, and carried both sets of figures upstairs to his office.

He quickly totaled each inventory list on his small adding machine. Then he subtracted the items which had been removed by his assistant and the supervisor. He stared at the final figure in stunned shock. His own inventory clearly showed hundreds of dollars worth of items missing. Impossible! Despite the tight controls he had put on the stockroom; despite the new door and the heavy padlock; despite everything he had done to prevent losses, the thief had somehow managed to rob him again. Now there seemed to be no solution.

Later that day, Walter and his equally puzzled assistant tried to figure out what they could possibly do in the face of such mysterious circumstances. Suddenly his assistant snapped his fingers. "I've got it!" he said. "Let's put an undercover agent in there with the stock people."

Walter hesitated. "I don't know if that's such a good idea. Don't you think it's going a bit far."

"Look," the assistant persisted. "We've tried everything else, and there's simply no way to find out what's happening."

Walter finally yielded and phoned a local detective agency. Three days later he hired an undercover agent to work in the stockroom. The young man was immediately accepted as one of the regular workers. Soon afterwards the thieves offered to cut him in on their loot, and the case was quickly solved.

It turned out that the gang wasn't bothered in the least by the fortress-like stockroom and fancy lock. In fact, they weren't concerned about the impenetrable lock. Their interest was in how the stockroom door was mounted. The hinges were on the outside, so with a hammer and a large nail they could easily tap out the holding bolts and remove the door. Thus they could enter and leave the stockroom without ever disturbing the lock.

In cases like this—and maybe not even as serious— restaurants sometimes suffer losses in which the best systems and supervision simply can't detect the culprits or stop the thefts. When this happens, your only logical answer is to hire capable undercover agents.

Difficult Job

An undercover detective is a loner and requires a unique personality. He must act his part completely, from the time he enters the restaurant in the morning until he leaves at night. He is hired to do a specific job in the restaurant, and he must do the job normally expected of the person hired for the position. But he also works at gaining the confidence of his fellow employees. Thus if his coworkers are stealing, his goal is to persuade them to cut him in on the action. Then he must find out the methods they are using and determine the type of items being stolen. If feasible, he should also try to learn how the items are being disposed of.

An undercover agent's job requires a combination of intelligence, analytical skill, puzzle-solving ability, and the talent to act out a role in a believable manner. But his main talent should be human relations so that he can win acceptance as a member of the group and gain the confidence of dishonest employees.

Costs and Ethics

A good undercover agent can be relatively expensive. Salaries for the most capable detectives range from $150 to over $350 a week, but an experienced agent is more than worth the investment. You should relate costs to cash recoveries, and when internal thefts are disclosed, the recoveries can be thousands of dollars. Often the expense of using an undercover agent may be minor when compared with the money recovered in a single theft case. One dishonest employee may steal anywhere from $300 to $100,000 a year from your restaurant.

Besides the cost factors, some food service executives are afraid to use undercover agents on philosphical grounds. These executives don't want anything to do with "spies" and don't like the idea of anyone being spied upon—especially at a time when governmental probing into people's private lives is a matter of great controversy. But management has an absolute right to know what is happening within its own company. *Ethical* means "in accordance with formal or professional rules of right and wrong." As long as undercover investigations are restricted to company objectives, none of the formal or professional rules of right and wrong will be violated. Management shouldn't want to probe the personal affairs of employees that aren't connected with business.

But honest employees have nothing to fear from an ethical undercover program. And since dishonest employees are themselves acting unethically and immorally, management is justified in ferreting out dishonesty among its employees.

Values Achieved

Some of the best ways an undercover agent can help your operation are to:

1. Detect thefts that can't be prevented by supervision or by the usual control systems and procedures.

2. Detect thefts in less obvious areas such as the receiving room.

3. Uncover "after-hours" thefts.

4. Solve the problem of a "suspected" employee by either clearing or incriminating him.

5. Uncover loopholes that dishonest employees are using to steal.

6. Probe areas in which excessive shortages can't be explained.

Thus the undercover detective can be invaluable in both direct theft investigations and in exploring areas related to theft. Now let's take a closer look at some of the main areas where he can help.

After-Hours Thefts

Workers on early and late schedules may find it easier to steal than those working regular hours if not well supervised. In one large New Jersey restaurant that baked its pies and pastries fresh every day, two or three bakers would come into the restaurant at 6 A.M. daily. Over a period of months they formed a collusive theft operation.

After a year the restaurant became alarmed by the growing inventory shortage figures and began an extensive security investigation. The study showed that items were being stolen late at night and early in the morning. Management finally decided to put undercover agents into various nighttime operations. One agent was placed in the porter group and another in the control division where a few night clerks and computer employees worked. Almost as an afterthought, the company added one other agent to the early morning baking crew.

In just a few days that agent discovered the source of the problem—the baking crew. Management was stunned by the extent of the bakers' thefts that were revealed. For almost a year they had been stealing on a large scale from the restaurant. They had even rented a warehouse on the other side of the city to hold all the stolen items. It took ten large trucks to bring everything back to the restaurant.

Cleaning crews are also a source of major nighttime theft. Such thefts often stem from a failure to screen the night porters properly before putting them on the job. In addition, because late-night workers are often poorly supervised, they feel free to steal with little risk of being caught.

Professional thieves, recognizing the lack of management controls over night porters, will try to exploit this weakness. A professional thief may contact night workers by starting a conversation in a nearby bar where the crew hangs out. He offers the porters immediate hard cash for stolen items. Soon theft may become the porters' main business, and cleaning, only an incidental consideration.

In one Miami restaurant where stealing had become an epidemic, management put an undercover agent into the porter cleaning crew. The agent discovered that late at night a porter would push his trash truck into a stockroom, making his usual pickup of refuse. After glancing around to make sure he wasn't being watched, he would remove several items and drop them into his cart. When his trash truck was filled with refuse, he would dump its contents down the chute to the baling room. There, another member of the gang would put all the stolen items into one trash bale and would put an "X" on the bale so it could be easily distinguished.

At the end of the shift, all the bales of trash were taken up to the loading dock and put onto a trash truck. The man driving the truck would stop his truck at a predetermined place on the edge of town and throw the bale marked with an "X" under some trees in a ditch. Meanwhile, the porters, after being checked off their night shift, would drive to the isolated spot in a pickup truck, recover the bale, take it to a garage, and remove the stolen items. Over a period of months, many of the items were stored in a large cellar at one of the porters' homes.

The undercover agent found that the theft operation was run by a professional syndicate. The group recruited employees and taught them ingenious theft methods. Losses from these thieves were estimated as high as $3,500 a year. If the restaurant had recognized the vulnerability of its late-night operations to theft, it originally might have planted an undercover agent as a permanent member of the night porter group. Then the syndicate could never have gained such a foothold at the restaurant.

Collusive Theft Rings

In recent years there has been a marked shift from individual to gang thefts. This shift obviously creates a more serious threat to restaurant profits. Sometimes the only way to combat this is with undercover agents. In a Portland, Ore., restaurant an undercover agent broke a theft ring in which a vendor's representative admitted cheating one chain of more than $25,000 worth of items. These thefts occurred because dishonest employees signed for items they never received.

Many years ago when internal thefts were mostly the work of lone thieves, undercover agents were not as necessary. Their crimes were a lot simpler. But probing into today's more complex thefts calls for undercover agents as well as closer supervision and tighter checking procedures.

The Suspected Employee

What happens when you have an employee who you suspect is stealing, but you have no factual evidence to prove it? Is the employee stealing or not? This can become a tense situation on both sides. Once a person is suspected of dishonesty, the tendency is to believe the worst. But the suspicions may prove unfounded.

An undercover agent working with the suspected employee can relieve your mind about the situation. Either the agent will quickly discover that the suspect is really honest and remove the cloud of suspicion from him, or he will discover that the employee is stealing, bringing the matter to a conclusion. This is far more efficient than pondering the matter and worrying about it for months without really knowing, and risking further unnecessary psychological and financial problems.

Probing High Shortages

Of course, inventory shortages can be caused by careless errors or factors other than theft. Sometimes the causes of shortages are difficult to pin down. When no other explanation is available, the tendency is to assume that thefts are at the root. Sometimes only an undercover agent can get close enough to the operation to find out whether the shortages are a result of theft, human error, or both.

By working daily in a particular area, the undercover agent trained in systems and procedures can often locate the source of high shortages. If the shortages are being caused by stealing, he can uncover it; if by carelessness and errors, he can find out where control procedures have failed. When a restaurant has excessive shortages that have resisted normal approaches, the undercover agent becomes the logical way to find the necessary answers.

Other Benefits

Besides finding the source of high shortage figures, the properly trained undercover agent can feed back a variety of information. He can help you by reporting on problems in employee relations, sueprvisory competence, and employee and supervisory attitudes. Details may also be learned about employees giving confidential information to business competitiors. Agents have been known to uncover executives falsifying company records and have solved such diversely destructive matters as production slowdowns, vandalism, and sabotage.

Establishing an Undercover Program

If you decide to use undercover agents, you might first try an outside detective agency. This would be wise if you don't have the time to choose or to work with your own undercover staff. But agency detectives are far more costly than agents employed directly by the restaurant. After all, an agency expects to make its own profit.

Some agencies provide talented detectives, well-trained and qualified for the undercover job. Others put untrained and unqualified agents into the restaurant who fail to produce needed information and create serious problems. You should investigate an outside service very carefully before making any commitment.

If you do select an agency, a member of your company's top management should work closely with that agency. He should ask the agency for a full report on the experience of the proposed undercover agent. This should include what specific cases the agent has solved, how long he has been with the agency, whether he has been screened for a police record, and what type of training he has received.

In dealing with an outside agency, the food service executive should spell out the information he wants and how and when he wants it presented. He should make it clear that he doesn't want reports on extraneous matters or minor rules infractions, and that he only wants to hear from the agent when the agent has significant information. He should also brief the agent personally on the background of the situation and the objectives of the investigation and should see that the agent receives specific training on specific procedures related to the assignment.

You can start with an outside agency, but it is wise to gradually develop your own staff. If the agents are permanent employees of yours, they will develop company loyalty. And the longer they work for you, the more they will be accepted by other employees. They will also become familiar with all the control systems and procedures in the company and will get to know a lot about management's philosophy and goals. They will know about supervisors and employees throughout the chain or restaurant and will have more insight into situations when problems arise. At the same time management will get to know its own agents and to understand them—what motivates them, how to evaluate their reports, and how to work with them to improve the overall operation.

In addition, an agent who is a permanent employee can be transferred from one job to another when the need arises. Employees in another department will more readily accept an established employee into their department than an entirely new one.

One vice president of a major Midwest food service chain observed: "When we used agency detectives, it was much more expensive, and it wasn't even productive. Sometimes it would take weeks and weeks for the agent to learn enough about our procedures and our people to give us any meaningful information. Now we are much happier with our own undercover staff, our own experienced and knowledgeable people. They know our employees and procedures and can spot irregularities quickly. They know exactly what they're looking for. On occasion we still use an outside agency for a particular problem. This usually occurs when we need an agent fast, to hit one trouble spot, and we don't have one of our agents who can be moved quickly to the problem area. On these special occasions an agency can give us fast action. But generally we find our own staff is more effective and far less costly."

Select Agents Carefully

If you hire your own undercover agents, you should exercise even more care than you do in hiring other employees. The wrong choice can cost you dearly in terms of failing to plug holes in your loss controls. Even worse, you might hire an agent who turns out to be dishonest himself and ends up joining the dishonest employees. Do a full background check and be sure that he has a perfect record for integrity. Bear in mind that criminals often seek security jobs and that as many as 25% of security job applicants have previous criminal records!

There are special qualities beyond basic honesty that an undercover agent should have. A role-playing ability is very helpful. Someone who has shown acting talent would be ideal. Often undercover agents must act or say things contrary to their real beliefs in order to become "one of the gang." For example, an agent who is an ardent liberal politically may have to put on an act and pretend he is a conservative in order to gain the trust and confidence of fellow employees.

If an agent finds he can't play an assigned part, he should be able to admit it. One undercover agent working on an executive suspect at a chain was sent to a convention in an exclusive hotel. The agent was well-equipped with a fancy wardrobe and heavy bankroll. But after his first meal in the hotel's luxurious dining room, he phoned his boss and asked to be relieved of the assignment. He simply couldn't cope with the glittering array of silverware on the table, help proffered by hotel managers and aides, or general atmosphere of wealth and sophistication—and he knew it. Fortunately, he saw immediately that he wouldn't fit in with the other executives and wasn't equipped to handle the role called for by the assignment.

An agent also should have analytical ability. Since he has to match wits constantly with dishonest employees, a sharp mind is essential. He needs to adapt quickly to emergencies and should have the talent to see how bits and pieces of information fit together. An applicant who is adept at puzzles, chess, bridge, or poker might also have the ability to meet and overcome challenges and to solve dishonesty questions.

The agent should also know something about the work he will do. He has to know enough about the skills required by the job to prevent arousing suspicion among the regular workers. For example if he is assigned to a department where most of the workers speak another language, he must know and speak that language if he is to be effective. He should also be able to communicate with them on their level rather than on some other, higher level.

Naturally he needs emotional stability and good self-control in the pressured situations that can arise. If he can't keep a secret or is boastful, other employees will inevitably discover his true identity. He must also be patient (as management must be, too) in this kind of work. It can take as long as six months before an agent can work himself into a position of confidence with the culprits and is able to break a major theft ring.

Contract Provisions

Even an extremely capable agent who has been hired on a permanent basis may have to be fired on a moment's notice if his cover is blown. To avoid any argument in such a situation, have the agent sign a contract specifying that he can be discharged without notice. Preferably, make it a two- or three-month automatically renewable contract. Don't ever tolerate a situation where you will be forced to keep the agent as a permanent employee regardless of what happens.

How should you pay the agent and still protect his identity? He should receive his regular wages in the same manner that his coworkers are paid. Additional pay can be given to him on a voucher, but it is better to pay him in cash. Submit a voucher through bookkeeping for some innocuous item such as "public relations expenditure." Either meet the agent personally to give him the cash or send a money order to his home. But be sure to keep the agent's extra salary off the official payroll, and don't let anyone in the bookkeeping department know about his identity.

Protect the Agent's Identity

If the agent you plan to use was an undercover agent in other companies previously, you should develop a substitute identity for him just in case anyone in your restaurant has ties with other operations that could blow his cover. This means selecting a fictitious name, background, and personal history. The name should be similar enough to the agent's real name so that he'll respond to it readily. Keeping his own first name and changing his last name may be the best answer.

It is essential for you to protect the agent's identity at all times. Under no circumstances should you ever reveal who he is to the supervisor of the department where you have assigned him. Only the individual employing the agent should know his true function. Even a top agent's effectiveness will be destroyed if enough people—even trusted ones—find out about him. Somehow the word will spread.

Once a supervisor knows an employee is an undercover agent, he will be curious to watch him and see what he does. He may even try to ask the agent periodically how he is doing. The supervisor may unconsciously arouse the suspicions of other employees.

Besides, a supervisor may be defensive about his department and his employees. Once he knows an agent has been planted among his workers, he may try to stop the detective from discovering any dishonesty in order to seem like an effective supervisor who runs a disciplined department. He may even go so far as to blow the agent's cover entirely by pointing him out to his assistant and even to all the employees.

When an agent's identity is discovered, there may be serious morale problems. The knowledge that there is a detective in their midst can cause panic and overreaction among dishonest employees. It could even result in such disruptive tactics as deliberate slowdowns in the operations. Or it might be used as an excuse by a labor union to call a strike on the grounds of management provocation.

The only way to protect an agent's identity for the months or years that it is necessary for him to build up his effectiveness is for management to select well-trained agents and to keep the situation confidential. The consequences of discovery or betrayal can go well beyond not finding the dishonest employees. It can sometimes even lead to violence. And it can mean a deterioration in the relationship between management and employees.

After an agent has left his assignment, management may be tempted to relax and reveal the true story of who he is. However, this should be avoided, since employees are not going to appreciate the fact that they were duped. Thus an agent shouldn't appear in court as a witness. Instead, management should obtain the necessary information from him to prosecute offenders.

To divert suspicion, if a group theft operation is uncovered in a department, it is a good idea to have the agent brought in for questioning along with the other suspects. Once he has completed his mission, he should be moved to a new area where he can furnish fresh information. It is wise to keep using this highly-paid specialist as a troubleshooter in key areas to gain a maximum return from his efforts.

Reporting Schedule

Don't expect instant revelations from even the most astute undercover agent. It takes time for him to gain the confidence of his fellow workers. The worst thing you can do is to put pressure on him for daily or weekly reports when he has nothing to say. He may feel obligated to give you some information and may invent stories which could be misleading and dangerous if you act on them. Instead, the agent should be able to report only when he has something worthwhile to tell you.

An agent should have the freedom to work for days or weeks without producing anything conclusive. Reports on minor rules infractions and other petty irregularities should be discouraged. You can avoid such time-wasters by limiting reports to the specific objectives of his assignment. This is an excellent way to save reams of paper and many hours of time and to focus on the main task—finding the thieves.

Guard Secrecy of Reports

One sure way for an agent to blow his cover is to be careless in writing his reports. He should never write anything if there is the slightest chance an employee will see his information. One agent wrote his reports at the local post office during his lunch hour every day and mailed them immediately. One of the restaurant's thieves got suspicious, followed him there one day, and grabbed the papers out of the agent's hand while he was writing a report. Naturally whatever effectiveness the agent had mustered up to that point was completely destroyed.

If the report is mailed, the return address should be a post office box or another prearranged address. It is too easy for an employee to connect the agent with his home or working address. And the agent should not make his reports in person to the boss. If an emergency does arise and he must see the boss, then the agent should have a good story prepared in advance if he unexpectedly encounters a suspect.

When using a phone to report, the agent should call at other than regular working hours and should use a pay phone some distance from the restaurant. The manager should have his own private phone to receive such calls to avoid having the switchboard handle them. Home telephone contact is even safer if urgency is not a factor.

An agent working in collusion with dishonest employees is in a delicate situation. For the agent's own protection, it might be wise for management to arrange a time schedule for the agent to phone in a report. If the agent is working in a risk situation, the lack of a report at the scheduled time could alert management that something may have gone wrong and that the agent may need immediate help.

Summary Points

Here are the key points in setting up an effective undercover program:

1. Opt for your own undercover agents loyal to your company; use an outside detective agency only in special or extreme situations.
2. Select your agents carefully for professional attributes—acting ability, analyticial ability, honesty, emotional stability, self-control, tact. Check their backgrounds completely.
3. Draft a contract specifying that an agent can be discharged without notice if his cover is blown.
4. Protect an agent's identity at all times.
5. Don't expect instant results. Have the agent give you reports only when he has definite information relative to the assignment.

Although there are problems involved in using undercover agents, management tends to overestimate the dangers and complications. A myth has arisen that using agents is tricky and dangerous. In reality, it is relatively simple if carried out in confidence using the proper guidelines. A well-planned undercover program can be your single most effective weapon in discovering and halting internal theft.

10

Interrogating a Suspect

Bill Evans, manager of a medium-sized Cincinnati steakhouse, stared at the report on his desk. Joan, a young cashier, sat across from him, fidgeting and quietly straightening her skirt. Finally, Bill looked up from the report and asked Joan, "Did you give your sister a lower price when she ate here the other night?"

Joan leaned forward and indicated shock and wide-eyed innocence. In a hushed tone of voice worthy of a star actress, she answered: "A lower price? That would be dishonest. I'd never do anything like that."

"And you say you've never given your friend Barbara Wilson any break on price either?"

The corners of Joan's mouth tightened in anger. "Who says I did?"

Bill realized then that the interview wasn't going to be nearly as easy as he had hoped. It seemed unlikely that Joan would admit anything, despite all the information in the report he had about her activities. Recognizing his own unpreparedness, he had the sense and tact to back away when he saw the situation becoming untenable.

He nervously cleared his throat and said, "Well, I just wanted to be sure. You know, Joan, we have to be very careful when we ring up sales for our family or our friends. If we make a mistake, other employees get suspicious; and you know how employees love to gossip. Just so that we don't face this question in the future, I'd like you to have someone else handle the bills of your family and personal friends. Then there won't be any danger of gossip among the employees that might damage your reputation."

Joan sounded relieved as she said, "Oh, I'd be glad to do that."

Now Bill smiled and took the offensive. "You will be careful in the future, won't you?"

"Of course, Mr. Evans. You know I'm very careful when I ring up bills. I wouldn't want anyone to think I was dishonest."

Joan firmly shoved back her chair, turned and left the office with her final words hanging in the air like a rattlesnake daring anyone to disturb them.

What had happened? Bill Evans' error stemmed from his misjudging the situation and not preparing for the interview. He fantasized about the interview and how it would go before asking the young woman into his office. This gave him a false sense of confidence. In his fantasy, everything fell into place easily. Joan would confess and would then blame other employees. After all, he would have total command of the characters, the dialogue, and the action. But the real world is quite different from the world of fantasy.

Unfortunately, a restaurant manager often knows very little about employee interrogations. A manager who can deal well with people wrongly assumes that employee interrogations take the same skills as daily human relations. He tends to underestimate the risks involved in interrogating dishonest employees. He doesn't realize that they may either try to bluff their way through the situation or cause a possible emotional confrontation. This has even resulted in court cases involving the restaurant and the manager. Some companies hire specially trained interviewers to conduct all such interrogations. Most restaurant companies, however, are too small to afford special interviewers. But court suits can arise form poorly handled interrogations, no matter who conducts them, so it is crucial for any potential interviewer to be completely familiar with the basics of interrogation.

The reason interrogating a suspect is so difficult is that you often have to prove innocence or guilt without having any direct evidence at hand. You usually haven't witnessed the actual thievery. A confession can be difficult to obtain, and you need extra skill in your questioning to do so.

Why Interrogate?

Before deciding whether to interview a suspect, it's wise to review your objectives in conducting the interrogation. What information are you seeking? Is the main purpose just to obtain a confession? You should not undertake an interrogation unless you have the facts and evidence needed to prove a person guilty in a courtroom. The only logical reason for an interrogation is to determine how the case can best be handled. Should the employee be discharged, turned over to the police, given psychological help, or forced to pay restitution? In addition, you'll want to discover an employee's theft methods so your control system can be tightened and your supervisory performance improved.

Your interrogation should seek as much information as feasible about why a person stole. Knowing how and why a person stole can be a great help in preventing recurrences of the same type of incidents. Here are some of the key questions you'll want answered during an interrogation interview:

1. Is the employee guilty or innocent?
2. What first gave him the idea of stealing?
3. When did his thefts start? What was his motive at first?
4. How did he learn the method he used?
5. How often did he steal? How much cash or food items did he average each time he stole?
6. Was he stealing alone or in collusion with other employees?
7. What other theft methods did he use besides the one you uncovered?

8. What has he done with the stolen cash or food items?

9. How much of it can be recovered?

10. Does he know of other employees who are stealing? Can he or will he describe these incidents?

11. How does he think thefts like this can be prevented in the future?

12. What does he think the restaurant should do about his case now that he has been caught?

13. What in the employee's mental, social, and economic situation bears on how you would dispose of the case?

Thus the interview hopefully would serve the purposes of exposing the dishonest employee, recovering the losses, and helping the restaurant improve its supervision and control procedures. But it would also be directed toward helping the employee who is in trouble.

Preparation

Before making any move toward interviewing a suspected dishonest employee, ask yourself whether larceny can be proved. First, money or something of value must have been taken away. Second, the restaurant must be able to prove that this was done with actual intent to steal. If you can't prove in court that the money or goods taken by the dishonest employee were stolen from the restaurant, you don't have a legal larceny case.

Since it is not always easy to prove these things, many restaurants will give the employee the benefit of the doubt on a first violation. The thinking here is that if someone really is stealing, either they will steal again and confirm your original suspicions, or your warning will be enough to deter them from stealing again and hazarding discovery.

If an employee has committed at least two apparent theft violations, you'll be sure your case is sound and will avoid the possibility of being charged with false arrest, defamation of character, or accusing an innocent employee of dishonesty. Besides, guilt admissions will come more readily, and you can often get a more complete statement of the person's past thefts, including the method and extent of his thefts and the activities of other dishonest employees.

A larceny charge in a criminal court must state the exact amount of money stolen or the specific cash worth of items taken. It is not enough to be able to say a theft definitely was committed and to present evidence. You've got to be able to prove that a specific dollar amount was stolen.

Here is a handy checklist of questions to ask yourself before deciding whether to interrogate an employee:

1. Do I have all the available facts, information, and evidence relating to the case? Are there enough facts to warrant an investigation? Is the evidence specific, detailed, and factual, or am I dealing with suspicions, rumors, and gossip? If the employee denies stealing, am I able to provide proof that would counter any claims of innocence? Do I have enough evidence to prove the theft in a court of law? (Remember that if the employee doesn't confess, you may have to prosecute.)

2. Do I know as much as possible about the employee before interviewing him? Have I looked at the suspect's employment card and reviewed it carefully? Are there any time gaps in his employment record? If so, do I want to question the suspect about this during the interrogation? Who are his references? Are any of them employees of my restaurant? (These names will be important if you later question the suspect about collusive thefts or his knowledge of other dishonest employees.) Did his former company give him a good recommendation? Have I telephoned them to ask questions that could uncover valuable information in a prospective interrogation?

3. After reading all the reports in the case, did I take the time to personally interview the undercover agent, the employee who talked, or any other source of the charges? Perhaps I can learn further details that may not be in the report. Do I have a clear picture of exactly what is supposed to have occurred? Am I completely familiar

with the entire situation surrounding the reported theft? What time of day was it? Does the undercover agent or other source remember what the suspect was wearing at the time? Where was the source standing? What aspect of the situation first drew his attention? (Related questions will suggest themselves as you discuss the incident with the source.)

4. If the reported theft involves manipulation of company records, am I sure that I fully understand what this manipulation consists of, what document was changed, how it was changed, when, and by whom? Was it rewritten or written over? Was it erased? Do I have available on my desk every document in question before starting the interrogation? In addition to the source of the report, have I interviewed other personnel from related areas such as the accounting department, cashier's office, or anyone who might have more information about the embezzlement?

5. Have I checked the actual documents against the reports? If I want to question an employee on the basis of a single theft because he had stolen money hidden on him, am I certain that the money has been properly marked and recorded, and that I know exactly where on the suspect's person the money has been concealed?

6. Have I questioned the person who reported the alleged theft very carefully to be sure he saw and reported exactly what happened? Have I separated the person's factual observations from his speculation? Is there any ulterior motive the person might have for making such a report? (It is unusual for employees to come forward with information about other employees who are stealing, so it is wise not to jump to conclusions too quickly when an employee brings you such evidence.) Do I have some method of cross-checking the validity of the evidence? (More often than companies would like to admit, a psychologically disturbed employee has destroyed the reputation of a coworker.) Have I gotten a written, dated, signed, and witnessed statement, prefer-

ably in the writing of the person who is making the accusation? Does the statement contain sufficient evidence to justify interrogating the suspect? Should I move an undercover agent into the suspect's department to get a firmer case before starting interrogation?

Each employee interrogation has a theft situation behind it that involves facts and information. Your task before starting the interview is to obtain more details. There's no need to rush the investigation. You can find ways to delay the interview until you have completed any necessary research. The suspected employee will be available whenever you want. So pick the best time of day, the best situation, and the best set of surrounding elements involved in the encounter. Once you take care of all the details before you confront the suspect, you can be more confident during the actual interview.

Coach the Witness

Anyone who is going to help you with the interrogation should also be prepared in advance. He should know what is expected of him. If you plan to use a witness to confront a suspect, you should prepare the witness and have him available at the time of the interview. It would prove embarrassing to reach a critical point in the interrogation when you want to call in the witness and find out that he isn't in the restaurant.

If you use a witness, you still should do all the questioning yourself. Any conversation between the witness and the suspect will destroy the interrogator's effectiveness, because it will ruin his rapport with the person he is interviewing. If the suspect questions the witness or tries to engage him in conversation, the interviewer must try to seize control of the situation.

By instructing the witness not to interrupt the questioning, the interrogator can more effectively hold the suspect's full attention. Let the witness give you a written note if he wants to suggest another line of questioning. This will throw the suspect off guard and give you added information.

Finally, be sure that only management personnel who are directly involved in the investigation, or people who have information to contribute to it, are present during an employee interview. If an interrogator allows any other personnel to listen to the conversation or allows them to be present during the questioning, this could later lead to charges of slander and defamation of character against the restaurant.

Be Prepared Emotionally

An employee interrogation can be a difficult emotional experience for a manager. He probably knows the employee personally and may be upset to find that he is dishonest. The manager may also get angry before the interview. (Employee thefts have a way of building frustration at all levels.) He may feel it's a reflection on his managerial ability. He may feel he has been betrayed by an employee he liked and trusted. Or he may simply be nervous anticipating the unpleasantness of the interrogation.

If you're the type of person who gets angry quickly, you might try breathing deeply. Invite the employee to your office, pause a few seconds, and take five deep breaths. You'll be amazed how this will relax you. In addition, try to focus your thinking on the employee. Instead of worrying about how you are going to look and sound, ask yourself questions about the other person. What could have led this employee into such a situation? What are his problems? What type of person is he really? Immerse yourself completely in trying to learn as much as you can about the other person. This will help you undersand the employee and what might have driven him to steal. It also will take your mind off yourself and make it easier for you to communicate without feeling nervous and uneasy.

Here are some of the common pitfalls to guard against when you start the interview:

1. Nervousness created by natural stress.
2. A desire to rush through the interview to get the unpleasantness out of the way.

3. A lack of self-confidence in your own ability to handle the interrogation.
4. Insufficient facts, evidence, and proof to substantiate the theft charges.
5. Poor timing, because you may not be at your peak of emotional, physical, or intellectual condition. You may have a cold or some other illness. Or you may have scheduled the interrogation at a time when you're being pressured by other serous problems in your operation.
6. Emotional concern and sympathy for the employee, and feeling of anger at or betrayal by a person you trusted.

Personal Philosophy

Before interrogating a dishonest employee, you should explore your own personal philosophy and sense of responsibility toward your fellow man. Failure to do this can result in a ruthless or thoughtless interrogation that can lead to serious emotional scars. An attack on another human being can be costly. The person you are going to question probably has the same fears, nightmares, complexes, and delicate inner feelings that you do. When handled gently and intelligently, the interview can be therapeutic and constructive. But if handled carelessly or with sadistic and destructive power, it can cause trauma and permanent damage to the employee.

So before you interrogate anyone, evaluate your objectives against your moral responsibility to the other human being and to yourself. Then try to achieve your objectives with the least damage to both you and him. To do this, you must apply *empathy,* or "the willingness and ability to enter mentally into the feelings and perspective of the person you are questioning, and to see and to understand the world from his viewpoint." *Empathy* does not mean *sympathy.* You don't have to approve his view or agree with it; you need only try to understand it. The interviewer's job is to try to assume the subject's internal frame of reference. He should try to see the world as the subject sees it, and to perceive the subject as the subject sees himself. The interviewer becomes a counselor and participates with the subject in the feelings expressed. He tries to feel them as well as observe them, and thereby absorbs himself completely in the interview.

If he feels an empathetic relationship, the subject will be more likely to experience emotional security and a feeling of safety. When he finds that the attitudes he expresses are accepted as well as understood, this gives him the confidence to explore his deeper feelings. For the first time he may see the antisocial meaning of his behavior. He will be better able to understand why he has acted the way he has and how he must readjust his behavior to free himself from guilt. He can then discover inconsistencies between his image or himself and what he actually is. But in doing this, an interviewer's accepting attitude helps him handle this painful experience and helps him see the better qualities of his own nature.

This ability to empathize, or understand how others see things, is not a natural talent. It is a skill that must be learned and calls for the most intense, continuous, and active attention to the feelings of the person being interviewed. An interviewer who tries to interrogate by a method that isn't backed with a personal philosophy is likely to fail. There are those who see interrogation as a chance to get some things off their chest, to get onto the pulpit like an old-time minister and give a sermon on morality. Others may have a touch of sadism under the surface and may actually enjoy punishing and frightening an employee. They see him as an object to be dissected, diagnosed, analyzed, and manipulated. They will express sadistic tendencies while rationalizing their approach as the only means by which they can gain a confession.

But unlike empathy, stress creates new psychological problems on top of present ones. It increases the danger of a major traumatic experience. Empathy, on the other hand, leaves the door open for future rehabilitation of the thief. It often results in an initial step toward better personal adjustment.

Fear tactics can also lead to a panic reaction. This may paralyze a person's ability to respond to your questions. Some people are so sensitive to fear or have such limited mental endurance that, when placed under severe pressure, they can't respond even when they want to. It becomes a case of mental inhibition. A thief in particular may encounter this problem or others; the very fact that he has stolen may indicate some psychological problem. An aggressive attack at that stage may destroy any hope of future adjustment and may have a permanently negative effect on him. None of us should want to risk this type of damage.

If you want to be an effective interviewer, empathy is by far your best method. But it must be genuinely consistent with your own particular attitudes toward people. Ask yourself: How do I look upon other people? Do I see each person as having worth and dignity in his own right? If I do hold this view at the verbal level? To what extent do I actually practice it at the behavioral level? Do I tend to treat individuals as persons of worth, or do I subtly demean them through my attitudes and behavior? Is respect for the individual uppermost in my thinking? Although I condemn a person's bad judgment in committing a crime, do I respect his capacity and his right to self-direction? Or do I basically believe his life would be better if guided by my ideas? Do I have a need and desire to dominate others, or am I willing to let people choose their own values? Do my actions reflect that I would be happiest with those people who permit me to select their values, standards, and goals for them? You owe it to yourself and to the employee to know your honest feelings about these questions before launching an interrogation.

Getting the Suspect to the Office

Once you've decided to interrogate an employee, you must be very careful how this person is brought to the office. It is usually a mistake to send an undercover agent to escort the employee. Although evidence may strongly indicate dishonesty, questioning may bring out the fact that there are extenuating circumstances. What may have seemed positive proof of guilt can turn out to have a logical explanation that can be confirmed by witnesses. This would invalidate any larceny charges.

If an undercover agent escorts a suspect to the interviewer's office by forcibly taking his arm, serious consequences can result. The subject may become frightened, which makes the entire interrogation far more difficult than it is if the subject arrives in a casual fashion. It can also cause the subject to panic and run from the restaurant, requiring extra effort to locate him and bring him back for an interview. In addition, it can give the suspect time to prepare a defense against questions that will be asked. Finally, employee morale will be affected if other employees resent the way the suspect is treated.

It is far better for the employee to be handled with courtesy and consideration. He should be brought to the office voluntarily, thinking it's a business matter, a discussion about some procedure or a review of some special assignment. Even if he has a slight suspicion that you may have caught onto his thefts, he can't be certain. Therefore, he will usually dismiss this fear. The result is that he doesn't anticipate the interrogation and doesn't have an opportunity to begin building a defense. Nor does he have reason to set up a barrier of hostility and anger. Now the interviewer will be able to establish rapport with the subject—a vital factor if a full confession is to be obtained. In essence, try to handle the apprehension of the suspect so that it appears to be an interview based on an apparent routine operating problem.

You yourself may want to escort the subject to the office for questioning, but usually it is best if a supervisor does so. First, however, the supervisor should be told exactly what the situation involves so that if the employee becomes suspicious, he should be cautioned not to allow the suspect to leave him even temporarily to go to the washroom or to his locker. If the suspect is a woman, she should be asked to bring her handbag with her. The supervisor should be advised not to indicate the purpose of the interview and to keep as calm and unconcerned as possible, staying alert to any possibility that the suspect might throw away money or stolen items on the way to the office.

The supervisor should exercise careful judgment. He shouldn't take the employee's arm or cause any scene in the restaurant which might make it look like an arrest. His conversation with the suspect on the way to the office should be casual. If the suspect asks why the boss wants to see him, he should say either that he doesn't know or that it relates to systems and procedures. The main point is to keep the suspect off guard so he doesn't realize the actual purpose of the interview.

Keep the Door Unlocked

When the employee arrives in the office, you must be sure there is no indication that the individual is being unlawfully treated in any manner. A "false imprisonment" suit can be very costly and damaging to a restaurant. Questioning an employee behind closed doors is walking on dangerous ground, because juries are sympathetic to the underdog, particularly if it appears that a large corporation is picking on some small employee. Sometimes a jury takes the view that a dishonest employee is the victim of a heartless, impersonal management.

To protect your restaurant from liability, when you reach the point of asking about actual thefts, you should tell the employee that any further discussion of the problem is on a voluntary basis and that the employee should feel free to end the discussion and leave at any time. You could close the office door during the interview for the sake of privacy, but *don't lock the door*. If you actually lock the door, a court may construe this as imprisonment. A major Chicago restaurant had to pay a substantial sum of money to an employee questioned in an office where the door was locked during interrogation.

It is also important to give the employee the impression that he can leave at any time and does not have to stay until he answers all your questions. Don't get trapped into making a comment such as, "Now just one more question, and then I'll let you go." The words "then I'll let you go" suggest strongly you are holding the employee against his will through either fear or force.

Whenever possible, try to conduct all your employee interrogations during normal work hours. This is more natural and arouses less suspicion. If an after-hours interrogation is unavoidable, be sure to have a second person in the room so that you are well-protected against any later charges of abuse, improper advances, or misconduct. If the employee being questioned is a woman, be sure a female staff member is present during the interview.

Taping the Interrogation

It is a good idea to tape-record all employee interrogations. This can prevent future charges and counter-charges based on poor memory or deliberate falsehoods. A recording can also be important if the subject makes a verbal confession and later refuses to sign a written statement. It protects the interrogator from future charges of abusive tactics or of threats and promises to persuade the suspect to confess. Even in a well-prepared case, there are times when an employee hires a lawyer and tells a totally fictitious story about being abused physically or mentally by the interrogator. He tells his lawyer that the interviewer threatened him and forced him to make a false confession. But once a lawyer listens to the actual tape of the interview, he will usually drop the case.

At the same time a tape recording helps prevent excesses by the interrogator. In the heat of the moment, he may use improper language and threats or he might make promises to obtain a confession. Any statement obtained from a suspect through threats or promises is useless, since the statement is obtained under duress. A tape recording can be used to prove that no threats or promises were made to the suspect.

Should the taping be done openly or secretly? This depends on management's philosophy. Surprisingly, the presence of a tape recorder doesn't usually inhibit a suspect. Still, some security specialists prefer to make these recordings secretly. But a secret recording of the interrogation may jeopardize future use of the tape. A secret recording is not suitable for playing when a suspect's attorney is questioning the interrogation techniques. And when a suspect knows his admissions are on tape, he is less likely to seek legal redress against the restaurant. On balance, the best policy usually is to make the recording openly and with the employee's full knowledge.

Equipment Selection

Choose a battery-operated tape recorder if possible. This is fastest and most effective, since it doesn't have to be set up in advance of the interview, doesn't have a wire that someone could trip over, and doesn't require a wall outlet. It is advisable to use alkaline batteries because of their longer life. But be sure to check them periodically, since they do wear out.

In choosing a microphone, one with an off-and-on switch controlling the microphone and the tape recorder is advisable. A voice-activated microphone can be used with such recorders to save tape, but these devices tend to be cut off one or two words at the start of the sentence until the activation circuits take hold. Also, when you later review the tape, you have no way of judging the length of pauses between questions and answers. These pauses can be highly important in judging the truth, amount of hesitation, or anxiety of a response.

Tape recordings provide a valuable training device for the interrogator. The recording is a permanent, reusable record of the session that indicates the coloring and emotion of the words as they are spoken. It shows where the subject hesitated or repeated previous statements, and it gives the length of a pause—particularly when a critical question was asked. This can reveal the mood and attitude of both participants.

You may find in replaying the recording that the suspect tried to confess several times, but that you were so carried away by the sound of your own voice and by your line of questioning that you ignored these attempts. By developing a tapes library of successful and unsuccessful interrogations, you can quickly improve your own techniques. Such a library is also helpful in training your assistant or other personnel so they can help you with future interrogations.

A review of a tape recording can also sometimes disclose important points overlooked during the interrogation that indicated clues requiring further investigation. If the interrogator must appear in court as a future witness, he knows he can easily refresh his memory by running through the tape—if he has been smart enough to record the interview.

Starting the Interrogation

When you begin an interview, it's best to start with some small talk; some questions about the employee's home, family, and job activities. You could consult the employee's application form in advance for help with this. You might try, "I notice, Joe, that you used to work for the K. R. Joseph Company. What kind of products do they manufacture? What work did you do there?" Or perhaps his hobby is photography. "I see that you like photography. What kind of pictures do you like to take? What kind of camera do you use?" Ask basic questions about his interests, and try to avoid questions that can be answered with a simple "Yes" or "No." Questions that start with "How" or "Why" are generally more effective, since they encourage the subject to explain things. To avoid emotional strain, stay away from personal questions about an employee's marriage, health, or anything that might set off an undesirable response.

Above all else, be sure to use the subject's first name. A person has heard his first name used by friends throughout his whole life. When you use it, you psychologically become an interested, concerned friend in the subject's mind. The one sure way to block easy communication is to address the subject formally as "Mr." or "Miss," which automatically establishes distance between you and the interviewee.

Maintain a "you" approach to promote casual conversation. Remember that your purpose is to encourage the subject to talk about himself. He may be a lonely, frightened, puzzled, or disturbed person. Since people are drawn closer to others with similar ideas and opinions, agree with him when you can. This will help win his confidence. People are like mirrors and tend to reflect other people's attitudes and interests. If you show genuine interest in a person, he will respond in a favorable way.

After the innocuous questions, introduce more emotional ones. Ask about his wife, personal problems, financial pressures. Talk to him about his children. But avoid any question directly relating to the alleged crime. Probe for emotional problems that might have upset his personality. Explore his social relationships and economic situation. These could help explain stealing and also might help later if you want to give him some face-saving reasons to tell about his thefts.

If the subject presses to find out the real purpose of the interview, you can stall by saying, "We'll get around to that in a minute, but first I'd like to talk a little more about you." You can then continue trying to establish a meaningful personal dialogue. By all means, stick to a planned strategy and don't allow the employee to frighten you into a premature introduction of the theft problem. If you allow the subject to change your plan, he will have taken control of the interrogation. You should remain in command at all times.

Feedback

After talking five or ten minutes, if you are at a point where the subject appears to feel free to confide in you, then you can approach the crucial part of the interview . Empathizing with the employee, you may now be able to get him to reflect back to you the personal problems that really may be bothering him. Much of this is a continued effort to convince the subject of your genuine interest in him and help him express his true feelings.

When you decide the time is ripe to move from the preliminary discussion to the specific crime, you must act carefully. Lead into the problem gradually: "We have noticed some problems lately concerning the failure of the cash register to balance properly when it is checked. You've had a series of cash shortages recently, and I wonder if perhaps you have some explanation."

Usually the employee won't have any immediate explanation to offer. You can start pressing him on how he handles the register on different days when shortages arise. He will start getting defensive. But you keep pecking away at these defenses point by point until the only obvious explanation of what happened is that he has been taking money.

Getting a Confession

The power of suggestion is a vital element in securing a confession. The suggestion must be logical and should offer sound reasons why the suspect will benefit by giving you the information you want. Thus if you suggest that "I'm sure you want to straighten this out and get it off your conscience," you should also explain why it's so important for the subject to get if off his conscience: that he will feel relieved and will no longer have guilt feelings.

If through empathy you have managed to build up a good relationship with the subject, he will usually accept your suggestions quickly. He will have a desire to please you and give you the information you're seeking. You can suggest that he may want to get everything out in the open. You can point out that there is enough evidence to go to court and prosecute him, but that you are trying to determine whether his behavior is a symptom of a psychological problem or some hidden pressure on his personality. Be sure he sees that you want to help him face the situation and find some constructive value in the interview.

To advance the subject's degree of suggestibility, you should try to remove fear from the interview relationship. Everyone has a natural fear of the unknown, of punishment, or of embarrassment. He may imagine all sorts of terrible things happening to him. Nevertheless, you should show him that you respect him as a person of dignity and value. You should do everything you can to make the relationship as safe as possible for the employee. Try to get him to relax. Provide a comfortable chair, and see that nothing is irritating or upsetting.

Usually you would combine your questions with a positive mental picture. But you can also weave in negative pictures with the positive ones to dramatize why the positive is more desirable. You might create a picture of the subject being taken to the police station, fingerprinted, shamed and shunned by his friends and his family. Contrast this with pictures of the employee walking out of the office free and ready for a fresh start. He has made a strong decision. He has come to terms with himself and can have his first night of uninterrupted sleep in months or even years. He will wake up rested, happier, and more ready to take on responsibilities and challenges.

Also try to be alert to people who are negatively suggestible. You could try this approach: "I guess you'd rather not review the method of stealing you used." A negatively suggestible person will respond in a contrary way. "Certainly I want to tell you about it, why wouldn't I? There's nothing I've got to hide." But if you had tried a positive suggestion on this person, he might have responded, "I took the money and you've caught me. Why discuss how I did it?"

Thus knowing whether a person is positively or negatively suggestible is vital in determining how you should formulate your suggestions. One way to test this at the start of the interview is by saying to the employee something like, "You can place your handbag on the desk." Most subjects will immediately lean forward and place their handbag on the desk. But a few, some of whom are negatively suggestible and contrary, may insist, "No thanks, I'll keep it on my lap."

In making a suggestion, think out the wording carefully to gain ready acceptance. Stay away from emotional words like "steal," "thief," "crook," "crime," "larceny," and "malefactor." Such words can set off a hostile response. Also be wary of bluffing. Your credibility will be destroyed and the relationship weakened if you try to fool the subject. You might find it difficult to reestablish the rapport which you have worked so hard to build.

If you expect to get the full picture of the thief's activities, you should try to make confession easy and painless. You can accomplish this by offering the subject chances to save face. If you give him a chance to explain why he stole, you make it easier for him to tell you the whole story. Don't indicate at any point, either by facial expression or verbally, that you feel he is a bad person; instead, take the viewpoint that he is basically a good person who has temporarily used bad judgment.

You might suggest some plausible explanations of his behavior. "Did you have big hospital bills? Did your spouse lose a job? Did you need money to buy clothing and things for the children? Are you supporting a sick relative, or do you have to take care of aging parents?" Such explanations can help him save face.

Usually this technique will work, and the employee will give the details. But if he still doesn't want to cooperate, you could say you'll have to turn the matter over to the authorities. Don't say "police." He will interpret "authorities" in his own manner, but you will have avoided an overthreatening situation which could have impaired his ability to respond.

Finally, you have a heavy personal responsibility in any interrogation. It may seem routine to you—especially after you've conducted several interrogations—but to the subject facing the theft charge, this could be the most traumatic experience of his life and might be a turning point. You must be careful to conduct the interrogation so that it doesn't inflict personal penalties or scars beyond those justified by the specific theft crime.

Remember, an individual's entire future is at stake. This doesn't mean you should relax your vigilance in protecting your restaurant's profits. But it does mean that in guarding against theft losses, you should strike the proper balance and maintain your perspective.

The Confession

If you can get the employee to admit the theft, detail the methods, and possibly agree on some form of restitution, you should try to obtain a written statement. This does not have to be formal. It could be written by the employee on a yellow lined pad. You could dictate the story of his activities and get the employee's agreement on each sentence before finalizing it in the statement. You can include specific facts from any agent's report and from other sources, as well as the specifics provided by the employee during the interrogation. The advantage of keeping notes during the interview is that they will now enable you to organize the material into a document detailing when the thefts started, why they started, and the specific incidents involved in it. The statement should cover the method of theft and the amount of money or value of the items stolen.

Once a statement is taken, you should let the employee read the statement aloud and ask him if he understands everything in it. If there are any changes he wants to make, have him ink in the corrections and sign his initials next to each correction. He should write, "I have read this statement, and it is true to the best of my knowledge." Then he should sign his name and address. If there are several pages, he should sign each page. Then you and another person who has listened to the statement should sign it as witnesses. The employee should also sign a promissory note, and the note and statement should be notarized.

Next, an assistant should have the employee empty all his pockets. A record can be made on a case history form of the amount of cash on the employee, plus any stolen items, locker keys, or other devices which might indicate all shortage sites for the stolen items. The case history form also should have the employee's full name, address, and basic personal data, as well as distinguishing physical characteristics such as any scars on the body, beauty marks on the face, glasses, or a limp.

The time at which the employee entered and left your office should also be noted. If you decide to prosecute, you should state the time the police were notified and the time they arrived. In addition, you should include your own name, or, if another person conducted the interrogation, that person's name.

Before deciding how to conclude the case, you should sit down with the employee again and further explore his private life. You should pay careful attention to the employee's present mental condition. Be sure that he is in stable emotional shape, or it may be unwise to let him go home alone. If the employee seems emotionally upset or afraid to go home, it would be better to have a member of the staff escort him home or have a member of his family come to take him home. It doesn't only happen in fiction; security files are filled with tragedies about emotionally disturbed employees who were allowed to leave the premises alone. In some cases, young people have run away from home; in others, individuals have injured themselves or even attempted suicide.

Immediately after the interview, you should write your complete statement about the case so that it will not fade from your memory in the next few months, when you probably will need the details. The statement should briefly review the method of theft, why the employee started stealing, when the stealing began, and any other pertinent information. This summarized review could prove extremely valuable in any later court action. The interrogator might end up testifying in court as a defense witness for the restaurant rather than a prosecution witness. A summary report written immediately after the interrogation can't be introduced as evidence in court, but it will refresh your mind before you take the witness stand, if the need arises.

The Consequences and Your Role

One of the toughest decisions you may face is what to do with a heretofore trusted, highly capable, long-term employee who is caught stealing. Not only are you likely to be shocked to discover that he is stealing, but you may feel that the theft is out of character for that person. Should he be put out on the street like any other thief? Or does his fine work record and long-term employment merit further consideration. Should he be given a second chance?

The answer is an emphatic *no*. You should *not* retain him. You should not risk any such temptation to be the good guy. No matter how mitigating the circumstances, no matter how sorry you feel for the employee, no matter how much you feel the restaurant—or even you—may be somewhat at fault; no matter what, discharge him!

He may sincerely repent. In fact, he probably will say, "I just don't know why I did it; I didn't really need any of those things." But the very admission that he doesn't know why he stole is evidence of the danger in keeping him on the job. The likelihood is that such a person will steal again, no matter how much he seems to repent.

Besides, keeping an admitted thief risks contaminating other honest employees. An honest employee who sees that you're keeping an apparent thief on the payroll—for even the best motive—may become angry at the restaurant and steal as an attempt at revenge.

The only exception might be a loyal employee of great ability who agrees to take a "leave of absence" after his thievery is exposed, who gets complete psychological treatment, and who has a psychologist vouch for his rehabilitation. The employee could then return to the job, providing he is watched carefully. But in every other case you must recognize employee theft as a sign of a personality disorder which can lead to further thefts if the employee is retained. I personally feel that most people don't change that much, although sometimes behavior can be modified.

When disposing of a theft case, the restaurant can terminate an employee on the basis of dishonesty, a policy violation, or a larceny prosecution. The choice should be based on the attitudes and policies of the company as to where responsibility lies when a employee steals. Is the responsibility entirely with the thief, or does management have a responsibility to prevent the employee from being placed in an unduly tempting position? The restaurant should always resist setting up any situation which can become an invitation to steal.

If you receive any request for a reference check on the discharged employee, you must be very careful not to reveal any details about the discharge. You may state the employee was dismissed for a rules violation, but don't reveal any specifics. You could explain that company policy requires such matters to be kept confidential. Under no circumstances should anyone say the employee was discharged for dishonesty. Since in most cases you have no factual proof that the employee actually stole cash, you could leave yourself wide open for a serious damage suit if you reveal any of the specifics to prospective employers.

Summary Points

Here are the main points to remember about interrogating a suspect and the aftermath:

1. Develop a personal philosophy enabling you to respect the person being interviewed as an individual.
2. Develop empathy by showing a genuine interest in the person you are questioning.
3. Maintain a neutral attitude, and try to see the subject's viewpoint.
4. Start by asking neutral questions which don't have emotional implications.
5. Learn to be a good listener; lean forward and show interest in the person.
6. Move gradually from neutral questions to the ones that may have more meaning and may bring emotional responses.
7. Then shift from emotional questions to ones related to the theft.
8. Help the subject explore the causes and results of his antisocial activities.
9. Try to obtain an admission of guilt by discussing why the crime was committed, and suggest face-saving suggestions to allow the subject to rationalize his actions.
10. Discharge anyone who has stolen from your restaurant and has admitted guilt; don't ever consider rehiring such a person unless a psychologist is positive he has been rehabilitated.
11. Don't place undue theft temptations in front of your employees.

Interrogation is an unpleasant task. But when things have reached such an unfortunate state, it is wise to know the right techniques to approach the situation in the best way you can. An interrogation session can be the most devastating experience an employee will ever undergo—but it also can have immense significance for you in terms of allowing a thief to depart with some dignity from the premises and of permanently removing this particular threat to your profits. Once other employees see that crime doesn't pay, they're far less likely to steal from you.

PART 5

Keeping Your
Employees Honest

11

Coping with Frustration

In a Little Rock, Ark., restaurant on more night shifts than management would like to remember, frustrated employees reacted angrily when cartons of important food items arrived for the next day's operations. They didn't bother stealing anything from the cartons which they were responsible for opening. Instead, they dumped many of the cartons into the nearest compactor. This was their way of getting revenge against a company they felt didn't care about them. They seemed to gain a gleeful satisfaction from the fact that the next day the restaurant would come up short on key items and the manager wouldn't know why. These employees were expressing their frustration in a way that actually cost the restaurant more than would direct theft.

If you can identify the problems that are likely to lead to such frustration and bad morale, you are in a better position to reduce or eliminate it. Here are some of the major factors that eat away at employee morale and can cause them to take extreme measures against the restaurant:

1. *Rigidity*. An inflexible manager who sees only one side of a story doesn't promote happiness among his employees.

2. *Fear.* If a manager intimidates his employees, they may follow orders, but they will feel bitter about it.

3. *Apathy.* Employees will balk when they get the impression that a manager doesn't care what they do or how they do it.

4. *Inconsistency.* When crash programs are substituted for long-range planning, employees get discouraged and confused at the apparent lack of consistency.

5. *Thwarted ambitions.* Employees need recognition to build up their esteem.

6. *Fatigue.* Cashiers or other employees who have worked for hours without a break aren't going to perform efficiently or happily.

7. *Language barriers.* If a manager speaks English while his employees speak only Spanish, a frustrating communications gap will result.

8. *Inadequate or broken equipment.* Nothing frustrates a person's work more than having poor or improper equipment.

9. *Audits.* When auditors come into a restaurant to check on the employees, it creates an atmosphere of mistrust.

10. *Lack of a true incentive system.* If a manager is judged purely by the profit of his restaurant rather than by how he treats his people, the results are disastrous.

The Results of Rigidity

The restaurant industry has been plagued with a particularly large share of employee frustration. This frustration is often manifested through high employee turnover and excessive absenteeism. It is not uncommon to find turnover rates running as high as 200% a year, and there is hardly a restaurant manager who hasn't had to pitch in when a key employee is absent. Executives of such companies sometimes tend to grin and bear this kind of problem. They shouldn't, because where absenteeism and turnover are highest, employee theft may reach epidemic proportions.

Excessive absenteeism prompted the manager of a California restaurant to throw up his hands in despair and concede, "I've had so much absenteeism that I've made a new rule. If an employee phones in sick, he must bring a letter from his doctor. It's gotten so bad that I don't know whether I can really trust my employees. I don't know whether the person who says he is sick really is." Such feelings are hardly conducive to good manager-employee relations.

Incentive Systems

Not long ago a restaurant chain in the South was paying each of its four managers $42,000 annually, including salary and bonuses. Yet the four restaurants had an average annual employee turnover rate of 365% and a proportionally astronomical theft rate.

Why the seeming contradiction between the high managerial compensation and the low employee morale? The answer was built into the system of compensation. Since the manager's bonuses were based solely on his restaurant's sales and profits, there was no incentive for the manager to improve his personal dealings with the employees. All sorts of problems were inherent in the compensation system. Just as soon as the company instituted a more balanced bonus system in which employee stability was rewarded, the turnover and theft rates began to plummet.

You simply can't build up a loyal core of concerned employees if the employees don't stay more than six months at this job, or if the manager won't allow them to participate in decisions or to express how they feel about things.

Techniques must be established for rating a manager so that his bonus is based on a combination of responsibilities: profits, cost, and his use of human resources. Under one such method, if a manager were to exceed a 33% turnover, he could be penalized for that amount. If he exceeded a 50% turnover, an additional penalty could be assessed. A 100% turnover could draw higher penalities, and anything much over that would be unacceptable. Presumably such a system would greatly curb theft as well as boosting morale.

Profit sharing should be an integral part of almost any incentive system. "Employees have to feel they are part of the company," said the training director of a major West Coast restaurant chain where profit sharing starts one year after employment. Employees at this company's restaurants apparently feel a great sense of fulfillment, since the theft rate is almost zero. In effect, these employees are part of the action and feel responsible for it.

More restaurant companies are starting to recognize the value of a so-called "fraction of the action" plan for managers. This means that each manager owns a certain percentage (20% is the most common) of his restaurant in addition to drawing a regular salary. If that doesn't act as a spur to involving and encouraging the employees of his restaurant, nothing will. Motivation for greater performance and better utilization of human resources is at its maximum when a manager has an actual stake in ownership.

Food service companies that ignore human resources in their compensation programs are asking for trouble. Giving rewards solely on the basis of sales and profits can alienate and destroy the most important factor contributing to growth and profit expansion—the employees themselves.

A system based on rewarding managers handsomely for earnings alone is a dangerous one. It means paying managers large bonuses for reaching specific levels of earnings as a percentage of sales or as a return on invested capital and ignoring the human element and other important variables. Thus the manager who is a "pressure artist" can achieve high earnings for a few years but will destroy loyalties and motivations among both the supervisory and nonsupervisory members of the organization.

A study of one major company showed that of 1,300 carefully screened managers hired over a three-year period, only about 50% still worked for the company a few years later. Sadly enough, most of those who left were the best ones, and only the weaker ones remained. So that company was losing the managers it could least afford to lose and keeping the ones it could least afford to keep.

The company's policy was to reward managers mainly for attaining high earnings levels. This encouraged the managers to put heavy pressure on their employees. The pressure led directly to hostile attitudes, constant complaints, and eventually to the destruction of the operation.

In this type of organization managers actually may exploit some compensation plans for their own personal profit at the corporation's expense. This is what happens when rewards are given for liquidating a corporation's human assets. Managers in such a system are driven by personal greed or by pressure from their superiors.

A vast exploitation system—an absolute monster—can be created in which supervisors are rewarded for milking their units. Such supervisors often are promoted every few years to a bigger location as a reward for their cost-cutting efforts. They continue earning big bonuses by converting the company's human assets into cash. These managers can get away with exploiting the company for many years unless they are kept at one location long enough for their actions to finally catch up with them.

Naturally, the impact on employees is far more positive when managerial compensation is based on their handling of human needs as well as profits rather than on profits alone. In any case bonuses should be paid for superior earnings records only when employee turnover rates are at least kept at a reasonable level. Any compensation plan which rewards behavior contrary to the company's best interests should be dropped immediately.

In short, frustration levels and theft rates drop appreciably at restaurants where managers are given incentive to motivate their employees and treat them as important, contributing individuals.

Warning Signals

While a frustrated employee can be dangerous to morale and profits, a loyal frustrated employee can be doubly dangerous. Take the case of Joe Jones, who started working as a counterman in a Kansas City restaurant when he was in his early 20's. He dreamed he would be a restaurant owner some day, or at least the manager of one. But now eight years later, he is beginning to realize that he will never be anything more than a counterman.

Bitterly frustrated, Joe decides to fight the system. Every night he carries a box of steaks out the front door under his arm and says, "Good night" to the boss, who returns the "Good night" and never checks the box. After all, the boss reasons, Joe has been there eight years and wouldn't do anything to hurt the restaurant. He is a loyal, trusted employee.

But Joe is frustrated. And by now he knows all the operation's systems. He has been there so long, in fact, and is so aware of the procedures that he can easily carry steaks out the front door without anyone's suspecting.

The solution to such a problem is not to promote Joe beyond his capability as a counterman, but rather to find extra tasks that will give him esteem. Perhaps he could be the editor of your employee newsletter or the captain of your bowling team. Or maybe he could be your representative at a restaurant conference in a town 40 miles away and report back to you. As long as Joe feels some sense of responsibility and importance, he will be happy. He doesn't have to be an owner or manager. In fact, if he couldn't handle these tasks, perhaps he even realizes it. He doesn't even require a raise or another title. All he needs is a feeling that he is continuing to grow in ability and responsibility and has an opportunity to develop and learn from his work experiences.

Fear

Fear of a superior is one of the major causes of employee thefts against restaurants. A fearful, resentful employee who is afraid to do anything that will directly hurt his boss will take out his hostility on the restaurant by stealing food or cash.

The kind of action that causes such fear and frustration is exemplified by one restaurant manager who spotted a dishwasher drinking a coke. The dishwasher had worked there six months and was a reliable, hard-working employee. When the manager asked the dishwasher whether he had paid for the coke, the reply was an honest "No." The manager fired him on the spot, telling him to get his pay and leave the restaurant. The employee's only comment to his fellow workers as he left was, "Next time I'll lie."

A manager who acts impulsively and harshly and who instills fear in his employees, hurts employee morale, loses valuable help, wipes out loyalty, and is detrimental to the overall food service operation.

Apathy

If there's one thing worse than a manager who instills fear in his employees, it's a manager who doesn't care at all. A waitress who had given five years of loyal service to a restaurant wept openly when she arrived home one Christmas Eve. "You know, when we all left work, our manager didn't even wish any of us a 'Merry Christmas,' " she told her family. She had wanted her manager to show in some small way that he cared about her as an individual.

And in another restaurant the manager was almost always in his office handling administrative work. "When things get busy in this place, the manager just sits around in his office," one frustrated employee said. "He just watches everybody else do the work." In neither of these situations did the manager display the kind of understanding or judgment that leads toward good employee-management relations and good employee morale. And when managers indicate they don't care about their people, it is one of the most effective ways possible of destroying loyalty and morale.

Inconsistency

Inconsistent management also will destroy morale quickly. Here we are talking more about the top management of a chain whose policies fall on the shoulders of the restaurant manager and his employees. Danger arises when a management makes a habit of suddenly substituting crash programs for long-range planning.

This kind of management forces its employees to live in a climate of crisis. One day it wants to cut overtime, the next day it wants employees to work longer hours. One day it wants to remerchandise the entire menu, the next day it affirms the brilliance of the menu exactly as it stands.

Lack of consistent wage policy is another example of the kind of inconsistency that can frustrate employees. Take this complaint from a waitress: "Good-looking new girls come in and get $2.50 an hour. But if a new girl comes in and she is homely, the boss pays her only $2.10 an hour. Some new girls are brought in at higher rates than I'm earning, and I've been here four months." Managers themselves should try to be consistent whether they go strictly by the company manual or set their own policies.

A top management that does not present a consistent, dependable philosophy creates an atmosphere of emotional insecurity and anxiety in its employees. Employees can forgive just about anything but inconsistency. Unless they can predict how their superiors will react and unless they can work with a consistent framework of long-range goals they won't be able to function productively.

Employees love to see a manager who is willing to pitch in and help with the work. It shows he is human. If you help clear tables in a pinch, you'd be amazed at the positive effects on employee morale. "Oh, Mr. Jones, we didn't know you cared," was the reaction of employees at one restaurant.

Fatigue

Fatigue can also cause frustration. Overworked employees not only make more errors than alert, rested ones, but they are also more likely to feel resentful at having to work extra hours. A cashier who is required to work hour after hour without a break keeps getting more and more irritable. If she has to work through an entire three-hour peak lunch period, she may start insulting customers and not want to listen to their questions. This could be avoided by alternating cashiers and giving each cashier at least a half-hour off to relax.

An overworked and frustrated cashier is likely to alienate numerous customers. And how much money do you think a tired cashier will steal from the cash register because he thinks he is "entitled" to it? How much will he underring on the sales of even his regular customers?

One assistant manager in a restaurant known for its conservative attitudes complained that he was working 75 hours a week without any overtime pay. According to company regulations, supervisors are not entitled to overtime pay. But the assistant manager noted that one of his subordinates, who also worked overtime, actually ended up with a bigger salary check than he did. Now you have a particularly unhappy supervisor. Not only will the long hours of work make him tired and irritable, but he will become more demanding and less tolerant of his employees, inefficient in his own work, and antagonistic toward his customers. Eventually his subordinates, who will have to bear the brunt of the assistant manager's anger and fatigue, will also become angry and frustrated. Had the assistant manager worked fewer hours, and had the restaurant worked out a wage policy more consistent with the needs of its employees, these problems might never have arisen.

The lesson is clear: Don't overwork your employees. Make sure they're rested enough to be enthusiastic, alert, and content when they are on the job.

Absenteeism and Employee Turnover

The general manager of one small restaurant chain in the Midwest confided that he felt lucky he had learned to be a capable cook. "Hardly a day goes by that I don't have to take over as a cook in one of my restaurants," he said. There's nothing much he seems to be able to do about it. If he replaces one absent-prone cook with another, the same cycle repeats itself.

Absenteeism such as this fosters bad morale by making other employees take up the slack. "I haven't had a day off in two months," is one complaint frequently heard in restaurants.

Frustration has a contagious effect, passing from one employee to another with snowballing thefts and inefficiencies.

Employee turnover can be even more costly. It takes anywhere from $200 to $5,000 to replace an employee who quits. This represents the time lost bringing in a new employee and having him learn the job. Even if you use the minimum figure of $200 in replacement costs, the total loss is staggering. Consider one large restaurant that has a staff of 112 employees and a 360% annual turnover rate. It would have replacement costs of almost $100,000 a year and theft rates even higher because of the rapid turnover, instability, and disloyalty.

The assistant manager of a Des Moines, Iowa, restaurant admitted, "Nobody in his right mind can work in a restaurant with the kind of turnover we have all the time. Our night crew gets $200 a week, but it has turned over 18 people in just two months."

A manager can prevent a lot of the frustration-caused absenteeism and turnover by learning to be flexible. You should view your employees' problems in gray, rather than strictly black or white, terms. Rather than merely issuing authoritarian directives, you should react to their problems in a sensitive, understanding way.

How's this for creating pressures and frustrations in employees through inflexibility? A waitress at one Florida restaurant sums up her work schedule this way: "My boss tells every person who comes to work that we must work any schedule, any hours, overtime, nights, weekends, holidays. We've got to work whenever he says or else we get fired." Any manager who abuses his employees like this is going to end up losing his best workers rather than his worst ones.

The same is true at a Dallas restaurant, where one employee reported: "We had a terrific cashier, and she was out for a month because her mother had a stroke and had to go to the hospital. Finally when her mother came home, the cashier could come back to work. But she told her boss that she couldn't work any nights and had to have Wednesdays off. The boss insisted that if she came back to work, she'd have to work Friday nights. She explained she couldn't because she paid a nurse to take care of her mother during the day, but she wanted to take care of her mother at night. The boss wouldn't bend, so she couldn't come back to work. Now she is working at a competitor's place. It's our loss and their gain."

A manager should judge a particular situation and show understanding when a loyal employee has a problem. He shouldn't be so rigid that he ignores the realities of an individual's situation. If employees know that a boss is flexible enough to understand a difficult problem, they will respect him more and feel less frustrated.

Audits

Auditors can also frustrate managers and employees. "They hire these guys to come in here once every few weeks to do an audit on our restaurant," recounted one manager. "I'm sure they're well qualified as auditors, but they don't know a darn thing about the restaurant business. They write up page after page of criticisms and make a federal case out of every little thing. Pages and pages of criticisms. They do nothing but find fault with everything in our restaurant. And they don't make a single constructive suggestion to help us to correct these problems." This kind of attitude creates feelings of helplessness and frustration among employees. It often makes them feel untrusted and suspect. Naturally, these feelings do nothing to further the cause of employee morale.

Language Barriers

Another major source of frustration is a language barrier between supervisors and employees. If supervisors speak only English and employees speak only Spanish, it is virtually impossible for an employee to express his feelings to his boss. The solution is not to hire fewer Spanish-speaking employees, but rather to have the manager or at least one supervisor who knows or will learn some Spanish. A manager who can speak to employees in their own language will find himself feeling less frustrated too if he understands his employees' feelings and needs, and will avoid a bandwagon effect of frustration among all the restaurant's employees.

Improper Equipment

Inadequate or broken equipment and poor methods of operation also contribute to employee frustration. Consider this complaint from a kitchen worker in a Chicago restaurant: "Almost every piece of equipment we have is broken. Either it can't be used properly or it needs so much repair that it's difficult to use. It's all junk, but we can't get the boss to either repair it or buy some new equipment. It's very demoralizing." When the boss doesn't have enough concern to give his employees the right tools with which to work, the employees will not only fail to do the job properly, but will also feel frustrated while trying.

12

Employee Discipline

One prominent Midwest restaurateur is convinced that it's about time restaurants stopped making themselves open targets for employee pilferage. "We've all been too easy in letting employees take food, candy, and liquor out the door," he insists. "There has to be a complete change of philosophy. We can't let employees get away with this kind of thing, regardless of their motivation."

He is referring to the friendly management "nice guy" method which some food service companies still feel they should use. This type of management depends on coffee breaks, long lunch hours, and permissiveness to keep the employees happy. It tends to look the other way when employees steal. But if you use this method and expect that employees will suddenly start doing their jobs more willingly, you're in for a rude awakening.

One major West Coast restaurant chain that tried this "nice guy" approach found that the employees became even more hostile. They reacted to permissiveness with sloppier work than ever. Carelessness and shoddiness became the order of the day. Theft losses mounted. Each time management took another step to "solve" the problem by being more permissive, the shortages climbed. Studies of the situation showed that the employees' main needs were for emotional job security. Management's permissiveness was working in reverse and aggravating their feelings of insecurity.

A general lack of employee discipline has cost the restaurant industry millions of dollars in both employee turnover and internal pilferage. When combined with employee frustration, weak controls become a potent factor in promoting theft.

Employee discipline is perhaps the biggest problem in restaurants today. Despite all your best efforts in other directions, there still are going to be some aggressive and frustrated employees. And these employees will steal if they sense they won't be caught. Good employee discipline can help prevent this.

What is employee discipline? Basically it is a set of clearly defined rules and penalties enforced equally for all. There should be no doubt in anyone's mind about these rules. Such regulations will give an employee more respect for your operation. He also will think a lot longer about trying to steal when he sees company rules posted and enforced.

In the context of a restaurant environment, employee discipline does not mean regimentation or a stifling of individuality. It means teaching employees to follow reasonable rules of conduct. Punishment should be only a last resort when all other measures have failed.

As one personnel vice president of a national restaurant chain said in describing his interpretation of discipline, "In our company, discipline doesn't mean strict observance of rigid rules and regulations. It means working, cooperating, and behaving in a normal, appropriate way. It means reporting on time, doing a full day's work, respecting the authority of the supervisor, cooperating with others, and, in general, acting reasonably and orderly. This includes obeying reasonable decisions and carrying out job assignments."

Although the need for this type of employee discipline may seem obvious, many restaurants ignore it. The experience of one Southern restaurant chain which encountered steadily worsening pilferage for several years isn't uncommon. The chain's executives couldn't figure out what was wrong, although it was clearly there for them to see. Reports from retaurant managers were being turned in very late or weren't being done at all. Many of the reports were found to be filled with mistakes. Nobody in the restaurants seemed to care about the rules, policies, or controls of the company.

This chain suffered from a lack of any real management discipline of its people. It couldn't hope to solve its shortage problems until it began to strengthen its employee discipline. Such a company would have more satisfied employees and far less theft if it could establish and enforce definite controls.

But how can this be accomplished? Any solutions must be understood in the context of an employee's need for emotional job security. There are four main facts to keep in mind regarding this, and all relate to the supervisor or manager:

1. The prime task of any restaurant manager is to motivate his employees. There isn't a single problem in the restaurant field that doesn't involve people.

2. Every employee who works in a restaurant has a basic need for job security. This need can be met through direct communication with his supervisor.

3. When a supervisor doesn't satisfy his employees' basic emotional needs through direct communications, he often creates a feeling of job insecurity among his workers. A dangerous emotional vacuum results.

4. A desire to steal from the employer may fill this vacuum.

But even when they recognize these facts, many restaurant managers don't like to face up to them. Managers often don't like to deal with emotional problems. They prefer to stick with the less difficult factual items to which they are accustomed. Furthermore, managers sometimes tend to be poor communicators. They tell or order their employees to do things, rather than discuss the situation with them. An employee is much more satisfied when he is permitted to ask questions and respond with his own ideas and suggestions.

Satisfying Employee Needs

Many restaurant managers and supervisors simply don't know how to satisfy their employees' job security needs. You can overcome this by keeping in mind four key areas in which employees need reassurance: job performance, job standing, supervisory treatment, job evaluation. In terms of these areas, employees would like the following questions answered:

1. What does my supervisor really expect from me in performance and behavior on the job?
2. How do I stand on the job? Is the boss happy with the way I am performing?
3. Am I being treated fairly and equally? Are all the employees being treated the same as I am?
4. Does the boss make his judgments about me on the basis of facts rather than opinions and assumptions?

If you want to prove how important these four points are to your employees, just ask yourself the same questions. After all, you're the boss, but you're also—or have been at one time—an employee. Don't you have the same basic needs and desires? Almost everyone at one time or another looks to his superiors to answer these questions and reassure him in his job.

It is interesting to note how readily we hold our superiors responsible for satisfying our own job security needs. Yet we easily can overlook or not recognize that our own employees place the same obligation on us. And unless employees feel a sense of security and emotional satisfaction from their jobs, discipline will be impossible to maintain.

Basic Rules for Discipline

It is a manager's responsibility more than anyone else's to maintain discipline in a restaurant. You've got to establish definite rules and prescribe penalties for violations of these rules. Here are some of the basic precepts to follow in order to attain the best working atmosphere possible in your restaurant:

1. Employees should know all the specific rules without doubt. Copies of all regulations should be posted on employee bulletin boards throughout the restaurant. They should also be written an employee handbook. Rules should be stated in simple language that can be easily understood by all employees. The restaurant company should publish minimum and maximum penalties for each rules violation.

2. A manager must take full responsibility in assessing penalties for rules violations. You can consult your superiors for advice, but you still must make the final decision in matters such as whether to suspend an employee pending a complete investigation or to discharge him immediately for a serious rules violation.

3. Before deciding on a penalty, you should gather all the facts and assess the punishment on the basis of a spread between minimum and maximum posted penalties. When you're deciding the extent of the penalty, you should consider the seriousness of the offense, the past record of the employee, the situation surrounding a particular incident, and previous practices of the restaurant in similar cases.

Discipline does not mean automatically discharging employees for the slightest offense. If you're going to enforce discipline fairly, discharging an employee should be a last resort. It should be reserved for only the most serious situations, where the offense is so flagrant that there is no alternative. Employee theft or an assault on a supervisor would fall into this category. So would a case in which there have been constant violations and all other corrective steps have failed.

It is vital to be absolutely certain of your ground when you discharge an employee because of the possibility of an appeal case. Of course, management should always be willing to have a discharge or any other disciplinary action reviewed by an impartial third party to see if the facts justified the action.

Your best employees are not going to be bothered by rules. In fact, they will thrive in an environment of discipline and responsibility. They may need a period of adjustment if you switch the working climate from being overpermissive to being disciplined. But they are likely to feel that rules and management discipline should have been established long ago.

When carried out properly and equitably, a tight set of rules substantially reduces employee frustration and theft. People really are happier when they are part of a disciplined, well-run operation. When you establish and enforce rules, you give employees the strong sense of emotional job security which they crave.

Post Work Schedules

Posting a work schedule well in advance for all employees and sticking to it is also an important part of employee discipline. Take this comment from a dishwasher in a small Midwest restaurant: "If it were up to me, there would be a definite schedule posted so that employees would know when they're working well in advance. But our manager just orders us to work whatever hours he says for that day. He doesn't give a darn about the employees. He just gives you orders, and that's it. If you talk back or don't obey, you get fired."

While most managers today aren't as arbitrary as this, it still is wise to post a full schedule for all employees at least a week in advance. This way employees don't have to wonder when they will finish work on any particular day. They will know how their families should plan meals and social functions. By taking the guesswork out of the schedule, you may eliminate some excitement in your restaurant. But by relieving the anxieties of employees and reducing their frustrations, you're making them less inclined to steal from you.

Package Checks

Should you check the contents of all packages that employees carry into and out of the restaurant? They might regard it as a hostile action, but sometimes it is necessary. It depends on your own judgment. The important thing is that there be a definite policy on this so that the employees will accept it. Try to be consistent: Either stop all the employees with packages or don't stop any of them. They will respect this.

In any case a manager should never accept a situation where he suspects food or other items are being taken out of his restaurant. This would have a bandwagon effect. If a few employees are getting away with it, all of them will be tempted to try it. In fact, most employees really want a manager to run a tight ship so that there aren't so many temptations.

Training Programs

Employee discipline should also include direct training to prevent employee pilferage. You should emphasize to employees that stealing is a serious matter and that it substantially hurts the company for which they work. Surprisingly often, employees assume that if a restaurant sells something for $1, it makes a 95¢ profit. If necessary, employees must be trained in markups and in the value of merchandise. They should be aware of the fact that restaurants usually operate on low profit margins, and that anything stolen hurts doubly, since what harms the restaurant also hurts the employees themselves.

Try to give employees a dramatic demonstration of the value of items. A Florida restaurant found that employees were taking beer mugs faster than the mugs could be replaced. It was deduced that the employees assumed the mugs were worth no more than a dime and weren't important to management. Solution: The mugs were prominently displayed for sale at $2.25 each in the front of the restaurant where all employees could see them. The pilferage stopped as soon as the employees realized they really weren't taking 10-cent items.

How to stop the constant pilferage of tiny items like sugar packets or matchbooks is a double challenge, because each item separately is *not* that valuable, even though they can represent a large total investment. You must impress on employees that stealing of these or any other items adds up and that it simply will not be tolerated.

Instilling good discipline in employees requires training, which is too often completely overlooked. There is a close relationship between morale and training. When a restaurant has a solid training program, it's demonstrating in another way that the company cares about its employees. It signifies that the manager wants his restaurant to be well-operated, and that each individual employee is recognized as an important contributor to the restaurant's operation and success.

A good training program at a restaurant shouldn't just include showing taped visuals on how each task should be performed, as many chains do. These taped presentations are fine, but they must be followed up by explanation, communication, and understanding. It is the manager's job to see that the theories on the tapes are implemented.

Summary

For effective employee discipline, remember that satisfaction is a prime motivating factor. Here are the main points to keep in mind when considering the best methods for maintaining discipline:

1. Aim to satisfy as many of the employee's security needs as possible. This includes keeping the employee well-informed about his job performance and job standing, as well as giving him equitable supervisory treatment and occasional job evaluations.
2. Inform employees of all rules and regulations.
3. Post work schedules well in advance for all employees to see.

4. Check the contents of all packages that employees carry in and out of the restaurant.

5. Indicate clearly the penalties of violating stated rules and regulations.

6. Assess a violator's punishment on the basis of how serious the crime is, the employee's past record, the situation surrounding the offense, and previous precedents in similar cases.

7. Set up a training program that stresses the value of various items in the restaurant and the harm that stealing can do to restaurant profits.

13

Types of Management

Security is like skipping a stone across a lake. You don't know if you'll make it or not despite your best efforts. But while the most elaborate security precautions in your restaurant are chancy at best, there are methods to keep your employees honest that can yield better results.

Wouldn't it be wonderful indeed if we could discover some magical way to prevent or almost eliminate employee dishonesty? Wouldn't that be a magnificent invention? It would mean you wouldn't have to frisk employees as they leave your restaurant late at night. It would mean you could sleep better at night, and so could your employees. It would leave you free to concentrate on the more pressing problems in your restaurant rather than constantly worrying about the threat of employee theft.

Yes, such a magical invention would be an ideal solution to the whole internal theft problem. But outlawing or totally eliminating employee dishonety is a utopian ideal. If an employee has a desire to steal or is thrust in that direction by various pressures, there is no foolproof way to prevent this from occurring.

There are at least 4,000 known ways an employee can steal from you. Even if you spent 24 hours a day seven days a week trying to figure out solutions, you couldn't combat all the possibilities. No matter what type of advanced control systems you adopt; no matter how many TV cameras you conceal; no matter how many security guards you hire; you are not likely to stop a hostile employee from stealing. You may put a dent in the typical 2.5% to 3% annual internal theft losses that restaurants suffer, but you will not be able to reduce it significantly.

A major restaurant chain in California poured $3 million into one of the most elaborate systems of guards, guns, police dogs, and hidden cameras imaginable. Can you guess what happened after that? Employee thefts proceeded to rise steadily. The employees saw these security measures as acts of doubt and suspicion by management. The moral: You can't go to war with your employees and expect to win. People simply won't be threatened or broken like this.

Besides, people who steal never really believe that they will be caught. Thus the young man who confidently walks out of your restaurant with at least three choice steaks under his sweater after his shift is finished every night takes the attitude: "Someone else may be discovered, but not me." Your best security measures are nullified by the fact that employees aren't going to worry about them. Cigarettes may be linked to cancer, but on the premise that "other people may get sick, but not me," cigarette sales in the U.S. have risen steadily.

Four Management Systems

There is a way to make your employees honest, however, and there is nothing magical about it. This method has nothing to do with security. It relates entirely to the type of management used by your company.

Let us explore the four basic types of management systems: authoritative-exploitive, authoritative-benevolent, consultative, and participative. Each system results from different attitudes and different expectations; each causes different actions and reactions. Some restaurants use one major form of management in organizing employees, and some use a combination of forms. By recognizing the consequences of using each form, you can decide which is best suited to the needs of your food service operation.

1. *Authoritative-exploitative.* "Just do as I tell you and don't ask questions or you're fired," is the essence of the authoritative-exploitative system. Management makes all the decisions without consulting the employee. Unfortunately, this system is more prevalent in the restaurant industry than we might like to admit.

In this type of working atmosphere, employees view management as having virtually no confidence or trust in subordinates. Top management makes all the decisions and sets goals for the company's future. These are issued through the chain of command. Employees face a working climate filled with fear, threats, punishments, and almost no rewards. Their only motivation is satisfaction of basic physiological needs. Any interraction they do have with their superiors is in a relationship based on fear and mistrust.

Under this system an informal organization tends to develop among subordinates in opposition to top management's control over the decisions and goals. This informal group will work intently against the goals of the formal organization and will strive to undermine the company in every possible way.

Rensis Likert, in his book *The Human Organization,* describes this management as having little confidence or trust in subordinates. He notes that under this system a manager seldom seeks the ideas or opinions of subordinates in solving job problems. Certainly subordinates would feel a lack of freedom in discussing their jobs with superiors.

2. *Authoritative-benevolent.* Under this system, management maintains a master-servant relationship with employees. Confidence in subordinates again is condescending, and the major decisions and company goals are set at the top. But some decisions are permitted at lower levels within a carefully prescribed framework. Rewards and punishments become the chief weapons to motivate workers. If there is any superior-subordinate interaction, management views it with condescension while subordinates view it with fear and caution.

While not giving employees a voice in decisions, management takes a benevolent attitude toward them. A manager will send cards or flowers whenever an employee is sick and will show personal sympathy or empathy to the employee whenever possible.

Here again an informal organization tends to develop below the top management level, but it resists only some of the goals set by the formal management. (Apparently management's benevolence draws more positive results—or fewer negative ones—than the authoritative-exploitative system does.)

3. *Consultative.* The third form of management is called consultative. Here employees at least have a chance to communicate with their superiors. Employees can express their ideas freely at individual and group conferences with managers. Employees can communicate with their superiors, but management still makes all the decisions. An employee can feel gratified that he has at least been consulted. Yet he still doesn't feel part of the final decision-making process.

Under the consultative system, management places substantial but not complete trust in subordinates. Broad policy and general decisions remain top management responsibilities, but subordinates are permitted to make more decisions at lower levels. Communications flow in both directions on the organizational ladder, and the company uses rewards, occasional punishment, and some involvement in managing the company to motivate employees.

A moderate amount of superior-subordinate interaction occurs—most of it in a climate of mutual confidence and trust. Management delegates major portions of the control process downward, creating a feeling of shared responsibility at both higher and lower levels. If an informal subordinate organization should develop here, it will usually support top management's goals.

4. *Participative.* Participative management means that management will meet with employees on a compatible and equal basis. A board chairman receives the same treatment as every other employee, although the chairman's opinions still carries more weight. Employees share in developing solutions to problems and situations related to their own areas of work.

In the participative process, management expresses complete confidence and trust in subordinates. Decision-making is spread throughout the company, and decisions are integrated for maximum effectiveness. Communication flows up and down but also vertically among peers. Employees are motivated through participation and management involvement and can improve their own methods of operation and appraise their own progress toward goals.

Such a company enjoys a steady flow of friendly, uninhibited, superior-subordinate interaction with a high level of confidence and trust. All units—from the highest to the lowest—are fully involved in the control and decision-making processes. Usually both the formal and informal organizations are the same, which means a total supportive drive on all levels to achieve company goals.

Economic rewards in a participative company are based on a compensation system developed through everyone's participation. All employees and bosses feel a responsibility to achieve the company's goals and behave in ways to implement these goals. There is a great deal of open communication and understanding between individuals and between groups in such a company.

As Likert sizes up the participative system, superiors have total confidence and trust in their subordinates in all matters. At the same time subordinates feel free to discuss almost anything about their jobs with their bosses. And their bosses get many of their ideas about improvements in the operation directly from these suggestions.

Results of the Four Management Systems

Experience shows that an employee theft rate for a particular restaurant can be projected within 10% to 15% based on the system of management used. This emphasizes how crucial it is for you to know what is the right management system and to be able to use it. I can come close to predicting the percentage of employees who steal from you once I know your style of management.

As you have probably suspected by now, the rate of employee theft varies from being highest under system #1 to being lowest under system #4. If you persist in maintaining an authoritative-exploitative system, you can just about count on the fact that 80% to 90% of your employees will steal from you. If you're a bit more progressive and use the authoritative-benevolent system, 60% to 75% of your employees still will steal. If you're much more progressive and have a consultative system, you still will face a 30% to 40% theft rate. But if you're smart enough to use participative management—where employees have a real say in decisions—your theft rate should be under 3%. You're not likely to get it much lower than that no matter what you do.

It's no surprise that the theft rate is so high under the archaic authoritative-exploitative system. It leads directly to employee frustration at not having any say in his company or in his own area of work and at being ignored as an individual. The higher the level of employee frustration, the higher the theft or loss rate. This frustration is manifested in one of two ways— and either way the restaurant loses. One is through depression, whereby an employee will steal as a means of compensating for feelings of loss and deprivation. The other is through hostility, whereby an employee strikes back in what seems to him a safe, indirect, aggressive approach. He may deliberately destroy customer relationships, steal from the restaurant, or do both.

What is the result of such an archaic management system? At one Midwest restaurant—probably duplicated at numerous others—the nighttime employees destroyed half the food items delivered by throwing them in the thrasher.

The authoritative-benevolent system, however, can actually be even more dangerous. Perhaps half the restaurant companies in the country tend to fall into this category, which on the surface seems like the easy way out of problems. It places you under an illusion that because you care about the employees, they won't steal. After all, they can look forward to receiving cards, flowers, and other symbols of affection, as the occasion dictates. But the employees probably aren't as happy as they appear on the surface. They don't want to be recognized only on special happy or sad occasions.

The major fault in this type of management is that the most serious problems still exist. When the employee sees that top level management still makes all the decisions without even consulting him, he feels left out and resentful. This is when he is most likely to turn to theft against the so-called "benevolent" company, which he feels has betrayed him.

Worst of all, a vicious cycle is set in motion under which the manager also feels betrayed, since the employees he treated so well are now stealing food and cash in return. The struggle may steadily escalate, and as the manager's hostility rises, so does employee resentment and theft.

In short, you simply can't buy the good will and loyalty of your employees. They want to participate more closely in the company they work for. Only through direct participation will they feel involvement and responsibility for the company.

Under the consultative management system, frustration and the theft rate are reduced somewhat, since the majority of employees feel they are at least being consulted. But one-third of them still seem to be frustrated because they are not part of the final decision-making process. To get rid of this frustration, management has to go a step further and encourage the employees to *participate* in the company.

A switch to participative management will not only curb theft but will also produce higher sales and profits through improved morale and efficiency. One food service company that tried to figure out why employee morale was so low and theft so rampant finally discovered the reasons. It was simply not tuned in to the sensitivities of its employees. After the company effectively switched to participative management, not only did its theft rate tumble, but its volume soared by 34% and its profits by 28%.

Participative management leads to higher productivity, lower operating costs, stronger morale, low employee turnover, low absenteeism, greater overall efficiency, a smoother running company, and less frustration and theft. It all sounds too good to be true, but it can happen. Under participative management, people come to work gladly because the job is satisfying.

Basic Management Premises:
Theories X and Y

Why is it that participative management is so successful? In part, the answer lies in fundamental philosophies of human behavior. Several years ago in a book entitled *The Human Side of Enterprise,* Douglas McGregor introduced two concepts of behavior. The first he called Theory X; the second, Theory Y.

Theory X holds that man finds work inherently distasteful. That most people aren't ambitious, have little desire for responsibility, and prefer to be directed. That most workers have little potential for creativity in solving company problems. That the best motivation comes at the physiological and security levels. Finally, that most people must be closely controlled and coerced in order to achieve corporate objectives.

McGregor's alternate concept, Theory Y, assumes that people are *not* by nature lazy and unreliable, but rather, basically self-directed, creative, and responsible in their work if properly motivated. Further, that motivation comes chiefly from the gratification of responsibility, success, and involvement in corporate decisions.

Clearly, the kind of management system a company practices will depend on which theory its managers hold to. Managers who believe in Theory X try to tighten control and closely supervise employees, relying on the idea that heavy controls are the answer to dealing with people. They feel that employees want to achieve corporate goals only if their own goals are affected, and this belief then becomes the basis of employee motivation.

Managers who believe Theory Y, however, try not to structure, control, or closely supervise the work environment. Instead, they try to help employees mature by exposing them gradually to less external control and allowing them to assume more and more individual self-control. They feel it is management's job to unleash the creative potential within each worker so that the company gets maximum benefits from his knowledge, experience, and ingenuity.

Generally, Theory X underlies the authoritative-exploitative and, in part, authoritative-benevolent management systems. Theory Y, on the other hand, is the basis for the participative management system, and part of the basis for the consultative type of system.

Participative Management

After years of observation and study, McGregor concluded that Theory X's assumptions about human nature are generally wrong and that a management system (authoritative of any type) based on this concept will not motivate people to work toward company goals. Thus managers who operate on the assumption that people are unreliable, irresponsible, and immature are not likely to be successful. McGregor concluded that management by direction and control is a questionable way to motivate employees. Drives for affiliation, self-esteem, and realization, however—those needs espoused by Theory Y—are far more important than mere physiological and security needs in McGregor's view, and also far more likely to yield positive results when tapped.

This is why participative management is so successful: It fully activates McGregor's Theory Y. The idea of participative management is to make the employees feel the company is theirs. Few people would steal from themselves or from their own company. Furthermore, employee involvement in the decision-making processes motivates them to find solutions to problems. Employees will do everything possible to guarantee the success of their own projects and will carry through these projects effectively. They will make life easier and more satisfying for themselves and for their manager in this kind of atmosphere.

Selecting Managers Who Operate Participative Systems

Considering that employee morale directly affects not only the rate of production but also the rate of theft in restaurants, it should not be surprising that managers of the highest-producing departments usually have the lowest rates of theft in a participative food operation.

High-producing managers tend to have the following at-titudes and characteristics:

1. They pay attention to important employee ego motives such as the desire to achieve and maintain a sense of personal worth and importance.
2. They recognize the employee's need for security.
3. They encourage curiosity, creativity, and a desire for innovative ideas and solutions.
4. They tap any and all motives yielding favorable and cooperative results.
5. They tend to engender favorable attitudes among mem-bers of the organization toward their peers, their superiors, their work, and all aspects of their job.
6. They do not rely on buying an employee's time or using control and authority as the coordinating principle of the organization.
7. Their organization consists of a tightly knit, effectively functioning social system composed of interlocking work groups. The individual in these groups maintains a high degree of group loyalty and mutual trust among members and between superiors and subordinates.
8. Rather than superimposed controls, they use measure-ments of organizational performance for self-guidance.

To be constructive, a manager should be sensitive to the needs of his employees. He encourages free expression and constructive criticism, indicates patience and openness, and allows others to take the lead sometimes. He should stimulate ideas and watch them grow, elicit employee discussion of prob-lems and solutions, and encourage employees to handle re-sponsibilities and decisions relating to an affecting their work.

Good managers often wait for an employee to discover the solutions to problems himself, rather than suggesting answers or solutions. They accept suggestions for ways of handling prob-lems and give their employees a say in the decision-making process. This way of overseeing, because it encourages a re-sponsible, independent attitude, diminishes the chances of pilferage.

14

Nondirectional Counseling

A middle-aged restaurant supervisor calls in sick every other day. Until now he has been one of your most effective and hard-working managers, so you are confused at his sudden unexplained absences. What you eventually find out is that his father is critically ill, and between visiting him in the hospital and taking care of his ailing mother and younger sister, he is physically and emotionally exhausted.

A previously reliable waitress begins dropping dishes and trays. Her absences become longer and more frequent. Then you discover that her fiancé has been postponing their wedding date for months because of financial difficulties, so she has taken another job to supplement her income. The physical and emotional drain on her life is taking a toll in her work habits.

Situations like this come up often enough to warrant attention in most restaurants. Emotional problems and difficulties can result not only in unproductive work habits, but also in mounting anxiety levels that can even cause physical harm to an individual who has no outlet.

Employees quite frequently have problems they would like to talk about with their supervisors. But only a handful of these people feel free to do so. This is unfortunate, since the way a manager handles employee needs has a major effect on the employee's job performance, motivation, and enjoyment of his job.

One of the most important ways of increasing employee morale is to indicate an openness and willingness to listen to employee ideas and problems. You may not be able to do anything about the problem at the time, but just your interest and concern may be enough to give an employee the support he needs.

This means, of course, that there are times when a manager must assume the role of counselor. In fact, employee counseling should be one of the manager's major responsibilities. Even when the restaurant itself has a professional counselor on the premises, an employee is more likely to go to his supervisor first, rather than to a relative stranger.

First you must recognize the relationship between an employee's job complaints and his personal problems. When an employee voices complaints about the job, he often is using this as a substitute for his own fears and frustrations about his personal problems. He will keep such personal worries to himself until he can either release his emotions verbally about "bad working conditions" or act out his feelings by stealing from the company.

A frustrated worker psychologically would like to react against the person who he blames—rightly or wrongly—for his frustration. But he will hesitate to take open aggressive action against any person in a supervisory position. Not wanting to risk punishment, he'll seek another type of revenge. He'll even the score in his own mind by stealing from his own company— something with which he thinks he can get away. Aggression and tension have built up inside the employee until he must find relief from the inner pressures. He may find temporary relief by expressing himself in the form of stealing.

If there is no verbal relief, the employee may not resort immediately to an aggressive act like stealing. But sooner or later he will feel the need to retaliate. It may come out later in destructive behavior against the person he blames for causing the frustration or against a safer target—the company. If the employee does retaliate by stealing, it is a subconscious act of revenge. He probably won't link the act consciously to a need for revenge against the company because of the frustration he couldn't handle.

When an employee comes to you with job problems he wants to discuss, he usually doesn't talk about the things that are bothering him personally. He'll present you with a long list of complaints about the job. But you must be able to recognize the real problem as an emotional one that has been building up tensions for weeks, months, or even years. Incidents on the job trigger the immediate emotional reaction, but the root cause of the problem may go much deeper. It is essential for you to find a way to curb the frustration, and that's why this chapter is so crucial to you.

Furthermore, as a manager or supervisor, you probably are confronted more often than you'd like to admit with the problems of an emotionally disturbed employee. How you handle such a situation will have a major effect on an employee's job performance, his feelings about the restaurant, and whether he is inclined to steal from it.

In fact, anything you do to improve working conditions in your restaurant or to reduce the amount of frustration among your workers is helpful to the individual and to your company. Studies indicate that at least 80% of employees would welcome a chance to speak their minds to a manager about a personal or business problem. But very few actually do so because very few feel free to speak up or criticize, according to the study.

You can't afford to rebuff any employee when he tries to express his anger to you. A frustrated employee who is blocked from expressing himself is an ideal candidate to start stealing from the cash register or smuggling out items under his jacket when he goes home at night. So you are well-advised to take any employee's anger seriously.

An aggressive reaction does not have to be a physical act like stealing. It can be channeled to something more constructive and verbalized. If his anger can be expressed in words, the employee can feel relieved and doesn't have to resort to a physical response. The challenge to you is to be sure the employee verbalizes his feelings and brings them into the open.

Employee counseling should be one of a restaurant manager's major responsibilities today. One form this counseling might take is *directional*, or giving advice. Under this approach the manager listens to an employee's problems, decides what he thinks the employee should do about it, and suggests a definite course of action.

But the best advice about giving advice is: Don't. When you try to give advice directly to an employee, it can backfire. You shouldn't try to be a psychologist when dealing with an emotionally upset person. No matter how worthy your intentions, such advice could be wrong and could complicate an employee's situation, making him even more emotionally disturbed than when he came to you for help.

Even if you identify strongly with a particular employee, you may still not understand all the details and innuendoes that are involved in the situation. Your advice may be not only confusing, but also unsuitable for the employee in that situation.

Instead, the most effective way to help employees with problems is through *nondirectionial counseling*; i.e., helping the employee to acquire more insight into his feelings and problems. This will help him to discover solutions to problems by himself—solutions which are more likely to be better for him than any you could suggest. Besides, an employee will more readily accept his own solutions that he has discovered himself than someone else's.

Listening Skills

If you want to be an effective nondirectional counselor, you should first develop the ability to listen carefully. This isn't as easy as it seems. Listening attentively to another person's feelings and problems can be exhausting. It requires concentrating on what another person is saying to you and trying to grasp the attitudes and feelings behind what is being expressed. It means showing genuine understanding and concern. It does not, however, mean involving yourself with the problem; once you do this, you will lose your objectivity, and with it, your ability to counsel well.

One inherent difficulty in listening is that you may be tempted to respond with approval or disapproval. This will effectively cut off all communication with an employee, since fear of negative judgment or criticism can frighten off an already timid individual. Norman Maier, in his book *Psychology and Industry* says:

"If a counselor or listener indicates doubt, surprise, disagreement or criticism, this at once places him in the role of a judge or critic. If he expresses agreement, pity, or even sympathy, this puts the listener in the role of a supporter. Neither role is desirable because as a judge he stimulates defensive behavior by the employee, and as a supporter he stimulates dependent behavior by the supervisor."*

Restaurant managers face numerous responsibilities and distractions. Thus you may feel circumstances force you to miss much of what the speaker is saying. Even worse, you may not be concentrating enough to interpret the speaker's true feelings accurately or objectively and may reach certain conclusions which are false.

To avoid these dangers, you must listen carefully to what the employee is telling you. Don't try to do ten things at once, or even two things at once. It's better to do one thing well than five things poorly. When an employee is talking to you, don't try to work on your calendar or run off a quick note to anyone or tackle any other kind of desk work. Any of these actions indicates ignorance and bad manners and gives the employee the impression you're not listening. And don't take notes on what's being said, since this often distracts the employee and halts communication.

Prejudices can also block communication. If you don't like someone, you will be less likely to be neutral and effective in your counseling. Try to be as fair as you can in listening to an employee. Try not to allow any preconceived notions about the employee to interfere with your listening. If you don't like someone, your mind tends to block out what that person says. Perhaps you don't like the way the employee dresses. Or maybe it's his sideburns, his posture, or some mannerism. Maybe you've had some unhappy experiences with this person or a

---

* From the chapter "Counseling and Interviewing," p. 598.

disagreement over ideas. Any of these factors can cause you to tune out what the employee is saying or feeling. Try not to allow this to happen. However, if you find this impossible, you should tell the employee gently that you are unable to be objective with him and suggest that he see someone else about the matter.

Nonverbal communication is also an important part of counseling. It can sometimes encourage or discourage an employee even more effectively than verbal communication can. Looking warmly and directly at someone shows you are interested. Leaning toward him a little may also indicate a desire to get closer to him and understand more intimately what he is saying.

During counseling, it's important to look relaxed as well as interested. Looking too relaxed, of course, will discourage communication. But establishing a warm, friendly, open atmosphere with your posture and expression will be an effective welcome for him. This should also help an individual to speak freely and without fearing that you will betray his confidences.

In order to be a good counselor, you should be able to go beyond what the employee says to how he *feels* about it. Part of this involves your knowing some information about the employee's background, personal life, position in the company, and aspirations. However, it also involves listening for *affective*, or emotional, comments, as opposed to descriptive ones. Suppose, for example, that an employee tells you: "I should have gotten that promotion. I've been working here for three years and I haven't even taken a sick day. I'm here on time every day and I'm a hard worker. I really feel that I deserve a promotion." Whether these comments are true or not isn't the important point. You could surmise from what the employee *says* that he really *feels* a need for more esteem or for being liked or appreciated.

Nondirectional counseling also involves acting something like a mirror. A mirror simply reflects what is in front of it without distorting or enhancing the image. Similarly, you listen and accept the employee's facts, arguments, reasons, explanations, stories of events, justifications. These you accept but do not reflect back to the employee. Instead, you attempt to reflect how he *feels* about the situation. Staying alert to what the employee feels, you listen to him and then summarize his feelings back to him wherever necessary to keep his train of thought moving, using slightly different wording so you do not parrot his words. Often hearing what he feels about an event can clarify the problem for the employee. In some ways it's comparable to a home movie in which a person sees himself and his actions quite differently from what he had imagined them to be. In the same way, when you reiterate for an employee his own feelings or arguments, he comes to see them with a fresh insight.

Let's say, for example, that an employee is telling you how he feels about a coworker. He may say: "Joe is just so lazy. He won't do his job in the restaurant, and everyone else ends up having to carry an extra share of the burden. It's really unfair." At this point he may stop and be unable to proceed. To encourage him when he has reached a deadend, you should feed him back his last expressed feeling. In this case, you might say something like, "You don't feel Joe is assuming his fair share of the responsibility." This is a neutral statement and lets the employee know that you are listening to him and understand his feelings.

He may now pick up where he left off and continue: "That's right. He never comes in on time, and he wants Pete or me to cover up for him. But I'm tired of doing that all the time. . . ." If he reaches another roadblock here, you might again reflect back his last feeling, summarizing it in a comment like, "So you feel Joe is shirking his responsibilities." This is a feedback of the employee's comment about Joe. Remember in reflecting what he feels to use other words for what the employee has just said, and to make your comments neutral in tone, not revealing any approval or disapproval.

Another typical nondirectional counseling session might go like this:

John Jones comes charging into your office, slams the door, and says: "I just heard you gave that promotion to Jimmy Doyle, and I don't understand it. I've been working in this restaurant for three years, and I've never even taken one sick day. I always come in on time and work hard. If anybody has earned that new job, I have. Besides, I've got a wife and three kids, and I need the extra money a lot more than Jimmy does."

Reflecting on this, a skilled supervisor would respond: "So, John, you feel you were not treated fairly in regard to this promotion." The supervisor has thus focused John's feelings for him and paved the way for John perhaps to solve the problem on his own. In any case at least someone has listened to John and understands how he feels. It would have been far worse if John had said nothing to his boss about how he felt at being passed over for promotion. This would have encouraged a whole cycle of hostility, resentment, poor job performance, and possible theft.

Or you can imagine what would happen if John's supervisor responded: "Too bad, I'm the boss around here." Surely that would ignite even worse feelings of frustration.

Take another example. One of your bookkeepers confronts you with this complaint: "I've been doing my job for three years, and nobody ever complained about any of my work before. Now you keep sending my work back and telling me to do it over. It just isn't fair and doesn't make sense. I make a few mistakes occasionally, but nobody is perfect, and I can't understand why I should get all the blame for what goes on around here."

In this situation the best type of reflected mirror response would be: "So you feel you are being blamed for not being perfect."

Or take the case of a young employee who has been working in your restaurant's kitchen a few months and comes into your office to declare: "I don't know why, but I'm just not one of the gang around here. I certainly try, and they're all nice fellows. But they have a closed club here, and they make me feel like an outsider. I'm beginning to think that maybe there's something wrong with me."

Again, the manager should reflect back the feelings in the simplest, most straightforward manner without passing any judgments. "Then you feel that the group doesn't accept you," is the best bet.

Reflective interviewing can be effective in calming down an emotionally charged situation. Take the case of a problem worker sent to your office by his supervisor. He starts off: "I don't know why I should be asked to talk to you about my work. I haven't really complained, and I don't have time for this kind of chit chat. So let's get it over with. Tell me whatever you have to say quickly, and let me get back to work."

What is your best reflected mirror response? "You came to see me because you were sent and not because you feel any need for help." Your reflected responses should be statements, not questions. And it is best to maintain a neutral attitude by presenting your summary-of-feelings statement in a slow, quiet monotone.

At no point should you pass judgments on a person's feelings. Let's say a young busboy tells you: "I want to get to the top. I'm not afraid of hard work, and I'll take a few hard knocks if necessary as long as I can see a goal out there somewhere. I don't care if I have to climb over a few people who might be standing in my way. Advancement means everything to me. I can't be satisfied with just an ordinary job. I want to be somebody."

You should pass no verdict on the merits or demerits of his case or his feelings. Instead, you simply can reflect back his feelings by observing: "You feel that you just have to be on top no matter what you have to do to others to get there."

Reflective interviewing also can be effective in letting an employee discover the impracticality of some of his own solutions. Suppose an assistant manager of a large restaurant came to you, the manager, and said: "You know, we've been too lax with our employees. If they keep violating our regulations, we ought to fire them. We've got to crack down with some severe penalties."

Using the reflective technique, you would reply: "Then you feel the way to solve our operating problems is to discharge anyone who doesn't follow the rules?"

The assistant manager may respond this way: "I certainly do. I can't do this job all alone. The other assistant managers have to do a better job. They're so soft that they won't fire anyone as our rules say. Once they let one person get away with something, everyone knows they can get away with it. The other assistant managers must stop making exceptions." But then the assistant manager himself might reflect further and decide: "Maybe the trouble is that the penalties we've prescribed are too severe in some cases. Perhaps the penalty is too harsh for a particular rules violation. It's very easy to make rules, but it's hard to fire a guy."

This is reflective interviewing at its best. You have allowed the assistant manager to reexamine his plan to discharge all rules violators. Once you succeeded in getting him to look at the situation again, he saw that his idea wasn't so sound after all. He obtained enough insight to approach the question from a different viewpoint. Now he is more likely to find a practical solution. Perhaps he'll suggest that extreme penalties for minor rules violations be reexamined and that firings in these cases don't make sense. He'll see that the punishment simply doesn't fit the crime.

When you start a counseling session with an employee, try to put him at ease so that he will feel relaxed. You might start off with some idle chatter about sports or the weather just to relax him and show you do have human reactions. Examples: "How did you like that football game yesterday? The Steelers really pulled off some upset, didn't they?" Or "Were you and your family snowed in during that big storm over the weekend?"

If feasible, sit on the same side of the desk as the employee so that the desk doesn't become a barrier. Don't allow interruptions or distractions during the interview, and shut off all incoming phone calls. You must give the employee your complete attention.

Questions Needed

Questioning is another important part of nondirectional counseling. In the beginning of an interview, it is important not to ask too many questions. They tend to lead and direct the conversation too much. They could change the interview into a directional one by channeling the employee's thinking along the same lines as yours. What is more, the employee simply may give you answers designed only to please you rather than to reveal his true thinking. Your questions could thwart open comments and expressions of feelings. Even worse, you could put an emotionally upset employee in a hapless position, since he may have no idea of the answers to many of the questions.

Instead of asking direct questions, you should be noncommittal and general. Bear in mind that your object should be to get the employee to express more feelings rather than more facts. For this purpose you can use neutral questions effectively such as: "Would you like to tell me about it?" "In what way did that bother you?" "How did you feel about that?" "Why do you think she didn't understand?" are all leading questions that open the conversation up for introspection and reflection. Also try not to ask too many questions that can be answered with a simple "Yes" or "No." This kind of question can sometimes lead to a roadblock and therefore defeats your purpose of getting the employee to open up with some comments and expressions of feeling. Instead, "why" questions generally encourage greater thought and reflection.

You can ask questions occasionally to keep the employee's flow moving, but don't interrupt him with unnecessary questions. The wrong question at the wrong time can interrupt or block an employee's whole train of thought. But the right question at the right time can encourage a person to proceed with his flow of facts and feelings.

Finally, questions regarding the outcome of an action can help an individual to explore various solutions or consequences. Such questions as: "What do you think would happen if you did that?" "Do you think you could eventually adjust to that?" or "How do you think that would affect others?" encourage a person to think ahead without directing his thoughts on the matter. This can often lead to the recognition of whether a solution is viable, whether it is effective, or whether it is merely a stopgap.

A good questioner can lead an employee to discover the most practical and logical solution for a given situation by himself. Recognize that the best solution is an individual one worked out in the context of an individual's own sense of values. Each person should know his own values best, and your main object should be to help him direct his thoughts to areas that are meaningful for him.

If an employee should ask you for any advice, try not to respond directly. The best tactic is to throw the question back to the employee and indicate he should be able to find the best answer himself. Some questions you might ask to parry the inquiry back to the employee are: "Would you like to tell me how you feel about that?" "What is your opinion about it?" "I think it would be best for you to tell me about it." "I'd be interested to learn just what you think could be done."

Although you may feel that an employee is on the wrong track, it is important not to challenge his statements or to argue with him. This is sometimes difficult to avoid, especially when you think you see the problem more clearly than he does. However, it is most important to let the employee come to his own conclusions based on his own recognitions and insights by himself.

Also try to remember that sometimes silence can be golden, especially during a question and answer interview. Silence at the right time can be every bit as effective as a whole series of questions and answers. If an employee is silent, you may think he has stopped communicating. But he may actually be thinking over the problem. If you can remain silent, you'll often find that the employee will start talking again on his own initiative. His silence is a healthy indication that he has taken time to review the situation in his own mind and clarify his thoughts. If the silence becomes uncomfortably long and indicates that he finds it difficult to continue, however, he may look to you for guidance. At this time, a summary statement or question might be in order.

Summarizing Feelings

Summarizing an employee's feelings for him in a non-judgmental and noncritical way often clarifies the employee's feelings. This involves your own attempt to comprehend exactly what the employee is telling you. If you repeat your understanding of what he feels, not only are you more likely to understand and be corrected if you are wrong, but you will probably repeat it in a fresh, new way that throws light on the situation for the employee. Moreover, if you summarize the employee's feelings in the same words he has just used, it might sound as if you are mimicking the employee, and that could destroy the counseling relationship.

Supposing an employee tells you: "I don't want to work with Bill anymore. He is lazy and has a superior attitude. He seems to feel he is just too good for this type of work and too good to work with the rest of us."

As a reflective mirror you should *not* repeat in your feedback statement: "You feel Bill has a superior attitude." Instead say: "You seem to feel Bill's attitude makes the work unpleasant." It's only a slight change of wording, but the meaning is there and it is probably more acceptable to the employee.

You can start off your feedback statements with such phrases as "You feel that . . ." or "You think that. . . ." But after a few such opening prefaces, you can feed back the entire reflected feeling: "Bill's attitude makes the work unpleasant." "You have to be out on top no matter what you do to others."

Your role is to feed back only the feelings actually expressed by the employee. Don't look for hidden thoughts or insist on figuring out your own interpretation of what the employee may be feeling. You should not try to diagnose the employee's emotional reactions, but rather listen and hear the feelings he states and reflect these back to him. If you listen carefully and selectively to what the employee says, you'll be able to reflect his feelings. Don't try to read between the lines.

If an employee expresses many different and conflicting feelings, and the time comes for some feedback from you, try to say something simple about what appears to be the feeling he has expressed either most strongly or most often. Again, be sure to say something about his feelings rather than the details of the case.

For example, an employee tells you: "I hate that Walter Jones. He acts like he knows everything and thinks he is better than anyone else. Sometimes I'm scared of him. Yesterday I went near his locker, and he shook his fist, threatened me, and warned me to stay away. He's a sneak too. You can't trust him. He's so underhanded. One day last week I saw him sneak out of work two hours early and had Bill Smith punch his time card for him."

Of all the feelings expressed, you would probably want to reflect back simply the last one: "You feel Walter is not reliable." If you tried to reflect all the feelings in the statement, it might just confuse the employee rather than helping him express more feelings.

Remember too that if an employee manifests hostile feelings against his interviewer, more often than not his comments result from his own personal fears or anxieties. It is rarely a personal attack. It may be that the employee feels inadequate in dealing with his supervisors. Or he may feel threatened by some of your comments or actions. If this is the case, try to understand *why* the employee feels threatened by you. Under no circumstances should you allow the interview to become a shouting match. If you find you cannot deal with the employee, terminate the interview until another solution can be found.

Set Time Limit

It is also wise to place a time limit on the interview. One hour is usually sufficient time to allow for discussion. If this is made known when the interview begins, the employee will know he has as much of the hour as he needs to discuss the problem. If the interview seems to be running on without end, however, you will have a reason to terminate the meeting without trying to find an excuse.

If a second interview seems in order, let the employee suggest coming to see you again. If you feel you'd like to take the initiative, do so in a way that does not threaten or push the employee. "If you'd like to talk this over further, please feel free to stop by at any time," is an encouraging but nonthreatening way of giving the employee the choice. If he says he does want a second or third interview, you should also try to schedule them at least a week apart. This allows the employee to think over and act upon what he has learned in the interview.

Summary

Here are the main principles to keep in mind at all times for effective employee counseling:

1. It is part of your job as manager no matter how much expertise headquarters may or may not have in dealing with these situations.

2. Don't give advice, but rather guide the employee toward reaching his own conclusions.

3. Try to make the employee feel comfortable and relaxed during a counseling session. Show that you respect him as an individual and are sincerely concerned about his problems.

4. Learn to be a good listener and concentrate carefully on what is being said. Realize that job complaints may reflect an individual's personal problems, and be alert to the employee's true feelings.

5. Be a selective mirror, reflecting an employee's feelings back to him so that he keeps spilling them out in the open.

6. Listen to the facts, but concentrate on figuring out the employee's true feelings.

7. Ask neutral questions that will lead the employee in a natural sequence from one point to another. Don't pass judgments on whether you approve or disapprove of what the employee tells you.

8. Help the employee explore possible solutions by asking questions indicating possible consequences of the solutions.

9. Let the employee decide whether he wants to come back for another session. Allow at least one week between sessions so that an employee's feelings and plans can jell in the interval.

10. Be sure the employee is always aware that what he says is strictly confidential and that he can trust you not to reveal anything to other people.

Nondirectional counseling is essential to a smooth and profitable operation because it allows employees to air their grievances or personal problems in an atmosphere of warmth and concern. In companies that practice nondirectional counseling, employee morale is generally considerably higher than in companies that do not encourage it. And employee morale is a must in diminishing security problems effectively.

PART 6
Conclusion

15

Future Outlook

When I think about predicting the future, I realize how inadequate I am as a fortune teller. Given a pack of marked fortune-telling cards, I misread the markings. On occasion I have been known to fumble and drop the whole deck!

My past experiences in predicting events have conditioned me to refuse to believe that tomorrow will be good golf weather, even if every professional weather forecaster assures me it will be a gorgeous, sunny day. If you are willing to accept these talent limitations, we can start our forecasts.

Before looking to the future, let's check on the past. As you look back across the centuries, ask yourself: "How much progress has man made up to this point in solving the problem of human dishonesty?" The problem of theft is not a new one. Through the ages, wherever temptation has existed, men have yielded to it. The human impulses that cause men to steal from their own companies appear as strong today as in the past.

When I think about the future, I wonder what man himself possibly can do to change the situation. Are there any answers to this problem? What new approaches can our criminologists, psychologists, psychiatrists, sociologists, and law enforcement agencies find? For years these specialists have searched for ways to influence human behavior for the betterment of society.

In thinking about how to reduce crimes against restaurants, I find myself faced with a roadblock. It seems to me that the first step into the future is sometimes blocked by the management men in restaurant companies. I simply don't believe that the first successful move to act on the problem must be made by the criminologist, sociologist, or psychologist. It has to be taken by responsible business leaders.

I am deeply disturbed when I talk to men in top management. I find they are sometimes complacent and indifferent to the crimes being committed against their own companies; crimes committed at the expense of company profits.

As I talk to these men—the men who should be most concerned—I feel like saying: "Internal business thefts are eating away your profits. They are destroying the foundation of your business. You must become concerned about dishonest employees, about the food items, and about the cash that your company is losing. You must abandon all attitudes of complacency and indifference."

Restaurant management undoubtedly is interested in better profits. In most restaurant firms, reducing theft is the fastest road to higher profits. Why then is the internal theft area so neglected?

A new method of theft prevention won't be developed to curb business crime until management wakes up and recognizes the problem. When a restaurant firm loses the battle against internal dishonesty, it usually has been unaware of what it is fighting, why it is fighting, or whom it is fighting.

Employee theft is an unpleasant subject, but it is one of the facts of life in the restaurant industry—a fact of large and ugly size. Employee theft cannot be totally eliminated, but it can be curbed. Companies can develop methods to thwart internal thefts.

Almost unconsciously, many restaurant executives think of employee dishonesty as part of the routine cost of doing business. They have developed a mental block against recognizing employee theft as *real* theft, simply because the thieves tend to be ordinary workers and executives.

When you talk to restaurant executives, you find many who frankly admit they don't know how much theft loss their company suffers each year. They will acknowledge some losses but show no interest in further exploration of the matter.

Executive failure to respond to the situation troubles me. I know most people read news magazines and trade journals. Articles appear in all kinds of publications telling of internal theft crimes. The evidence is all around and continues to accumulate. Yet the average executive refuses to believe it. He wears rose-colored glasses. I find he also refuses to recognize any relationship between the employee thefts he reads about and similar dangers within his own restaurants.

The harm growing out of internal theft cannot be measured easily. It means higher costs for the consumer, lower purchasing power for the worker. For some restaurant firms, it means outright bankruptcy, especially during periods of general economic problems.

The cancer of dishonesty suggests the collapse of American ethical codes of conduct. And management breeds increasing dishonesty by poor business practices, inadequate controls, weak supervision, and unrealistic policies. As we focus on the future, we can't ignore the present. The handwriting is on the wall for every restaurant executive to see.

Ethics Code Needed

One of the far-fetched ideas that still could come true in the future is the possibility that man will be able to communicate through mental telepathy. People will no longer need to use words. They will communicate directly from one mind to another. If such an ability is developed, stealing would become difficult if not impossible. A man with mental images of theft in his brain would transmit these pictures to all the alert brains in his area. This would be like a red dome light on a police car flashing a warning signal. The thief's own dishonest plans would prove his undoing. (Of course, to counter this someone might invent a portable "static-machine" you could carry with you so that your thoughts would become scrambled or blocked off from the minds of others.)

Mental telepathy may be a science fiction dream, but I'm convinced there is one serious need man must fulfill if there is to be a halt to internal theft and crime. This is our need today for a new philosophy of life—a philosophy that can be accepted by mankind. One which contains a workable and believable code of ethical conduct.

Two major philosophies dominate the world, and neither does much to reassure man. Instead, they leave him a lonely and frightened being in search of his soul. Both of the philosophies reject the idea of ethics entirely.

One, a scientific philosophy, teaches that only those things which can be proven true by scientific tests are valid. Ethical conduct doesn't have a reality within the scope of such a definition. The other, existentialism, teaches that man is nothing; that he is a lost being who has come from nowhere and that he will return at any moment. Obviously there is no ethical code for man to use as a yeardstick under this set of values.

No real progress in turning back the tide of future crime is likely until a majority of human beings everywhere comes to believe in a new philosophy with a code of ethics that stops all types of criminal acts. What can be done today to begin living according to new standards?

In realistic terms, executives must recognize that people who work for them are human beings subject to human frailities. This includes the inability at times to resist temptation. Therefore, one method of protecting ourselves against loss is to have systems and controls that protect employees from themselves.

But we also must develop in our employees a profound consciousness of their responsibilities. And we must make them feel important as individuals. We must listen to their problems and help them express the hostility and frustration which often makes them turn to stealing. We must make them feel in effect that *our* restaurant is *their* restaurant.

In helping the employee feel pride in his own work and in his restaurant and in eliminating situations of undue temptation, we can greatly reduce our theft losses and gain peace of mind ourselves. With these approaches, we not only protect our employees from possible personal tragedy, but we make it easier for them to preserve their own personal integrity, human dignity, and self-respect.

What could be more worthwhile for us to pursue than the twin goals of employee theft prevention and keeping our employees honest? These help us achieve both our own profit objectives and upholding high human values.

Bibliography

Bandura, A. *Principles of Behavior Modification.* New York: Holt, Rinehart & Winston, Inc., 1969.

Catania, C. A. *Contemporary Research in Operant Behavior.* Glenview, Illinois: Scott Foresman & Co., 1968.

Clark, Ramsey. *Crime in America.* New York: Simon & Schuster, 1970.

Combs, Arthur W., Avila, Donald L., and Purkey, William W. *Helping Relationships.* Boston: Allyn & Bacon, Inc., 1973.

Drucker, Peter F. *The Practice of Management.* New York: Harper & Row Publishers, Inc., 1954.

Erikson, Erik H. *Insight and Responsibility.* New York: W. W. Norton & Co., 1964.

Gardner, John W. *Self-Renewal.* New York: Harper & Row Publishers, Inc., 1964.

Hall, Edward T. *The Hidden Dimension.* New York: Doubleday & Co., 1969.

Harris, Thomas A. *I'm OK–You're OK: A Practical Guide to Transactional Analysis.* New York: Harper & Row Publishers, Inc., 1969.

Honderich, Ted. *Punishment: The Supposed Justification.* New York: Harcourt Brace Jovanovich, Inc., 1970.

Kotschevar, Lindal H. *Quantity Food Purchasing.* New York: John Wiley, 1961.

Laird, Donald A. and Laird, Eleanor C. *The New Psychology of Leadership.* New York: McGraw Hill, Inc., 1956.

Lazzaro, Victor. *Systems and Procedures: A Handbook for Business & Industry.* Englewood Cliffs, New Jersey: Prentice-Hall, Inc., 1968.

Lecky, Prescott. *Self-Consistency: A Theory of Personality.* New York:Anchor Books, 1968.

Likert, Rensis. *The Human Organization: Its Management & Value.* New York: McGraw Hill, Inc., 1967.

Maier, Norman R. *Psychology in Industry.* Boston: Houghton Mifflin & Co., 1955.

Maslow, Abraham. *The Farther Reaches of Human Nature.* New York: Viking Press, 1971.

Menninger, Karl. *The Crime of Punishment.* New York: Hawthorne Books, 1973.

Menninger, Karl. *Whatever Became of Skin?* New York: Hawthorne Books, 1973.

McGregor, Douglas. *The Human Side of Enterprise.* New York: McGraw Hill, Inc., 1960.

McGregor, Douglas. *The Professional Manager.* New York: McGraw Hill, Inc., 1967.

Rogers, Carl R. *Counseling and Psychotherapy.* Boston: Houghton Mifflin & Co., 1942.

Rogers, Carl. R. *On Becoming a Person.* Boston: Houghton Mifflin & Co., 1970.

Selye, Hans. *Stress Without Distress.* Toronto, Canada: McCleeland & Stewart, Ltd., 1974.

Skinner, B. F. *Beyond Freedom and Dignity.* New York: Alfred A. Knopf, 1971.

Toffler, Alvin. *Future Shock.* New York: Random House, 1970.

Ulrich, Roger. *Control of Human Behavior, Volumes I, II, and III.* Glenview, Illinois: Scott Foresman & Co., 1966, 1970, 1974.

Index

219